Letters FROM THE Last Pope

Sept 2022
To LtC VW—
my hero in
the highest echelons
of emergency response—
Semper Fi
Always
CPT [illegible]

A
JOURNEY
HOME

Letters FROM THE Last Pope

PHOEBE ELIZABETH POPE SISK

Letters from the Last Pope
A Journey Home

ISBN 978-1-5445-3260-8 Hardcover
978-1-5445-3261-5 Paperback
978-1-5445-3262-2 Ebook

CONTENTS

PREFACE ... ix

CHAPTER 1
Dear Kwalimu ... 1

CHAPTER 2
Dear Reader ... 11

CHAPTER 3
Dear Mama ... 21

CHAPTER 4
Dear House at Benbrook Boulevard ... 39

CHAPTER 5
Dear Man on the Street Bench ... 57

CHAPTER 6
Dear Dad ... 63

CHAPTER 7
Dear Patricia ... 79

CHAPTER 8
Dear Johnny ... 91

CHAPTER 9
Dear Taos Land 97

CHAPTER 10
Dear Abigail 103

CHAPTER 11
Dear Beatrice 109

CHAPTER 12
Dear Papa 113

CHAPTER 13
Dear Kate 119

CHAPTER 14
Dear Jody 129

CHAPTER 15
Dear Peter 135

CHAPTER 16
Dear Steph 139

CHAPTER 17
Dear Ben 145

CHAPTER 18
Dear Three Popes 157

CHAPTER 19
Dear God 179

CHAPTER 20
Dear Betty Carter | Dear Straw Man 183

CHAPTER 21
Dear Kevin 187

CHAPTER 22
Dear Sisk Family 197

CHAPTER 23
Dear Elijah 205

CHAPTER 24
Dear Sarah Katherine 213

CHAPTER 25
Dear Teens and Parents 223
Teach Your Parents Well

CHAPTER 26
Dear Veterans 239

CHAPTER 27
Dear Phoebe, the Day Is Good 259

AFTERWORD 267
For Phoebe: Kevin's Story
A Letter from Sarah Katherine to Her Mother, Phoebe
A Note from Elijah to Mom, Phoebe

ENDNOTES 273

PREFACE

Like most stories, mine has been under the surface, waiting to rise like dry bones, ever since my mother committed suicide forty-eight years ago when I was five years old. I grew up the youngest of my mother's ten children, impoverished by a lack of means—but never by a lack of love or creativity.

After my mother lost her sanity and her life due to the traumatic aftermath of a wrongful hysterectomy, my father raised us remaining younger children—several of whom were born to her first two husbands. As an artist, my father spent much of his time in the shop creating, doing his best to release the sorrows of lost love, while we children struggled in our own ways to heal a maternal wound that would mark our family for generations.

Research on epigenetics shows that we carry the trauma of our ancestors in our bodies. Therefore, it is to the benefit of *all of us* to collectively heal through a movement of intentional awareness, radical compassion, and personal transformation.

My book, *Letters from the Last Pope*, is about this movement.

The following chapters are a series of twenty-six letters to the most important teachers in my life—and while most are beloved, some are not. Through the retelling of life chapters with my siblings, I commemorate Mama—the haunting, maternal longing for the divine that moved through all of us . . . before leaving us entirely by her own hand.

While the toll my mother's suicide took on us as her children was obvious, less obvious is the impact it will have on our offspring, the succeeding generations. As the seeds of my children were alive inside of my mother after I was fully formed in her body, their lineage is also sealed in the womb of Mama. This book is about that lineage.

It explores the shared grief we experience as a people and how it manifests on a global level and into our collective futures when left unhealed.

While on active duty as a US Marine Corps officer, I experienced a life-threatening ectopic pregnancy. Like other military spouses, I faced this traumatic loss alone—as my husband was deployed and would not return until six months later.

This experience, paired with the tragedy of the imposed hysterectomy that stole my mother's mind, incited in me a lifetime of understanding the link between our psychological and physical health, as well as a need to seek a solution for spiritual wholeness following acute personal loss.

My story, like others of my era, showcases the expression of those who grew up in the 1970s, and how it has fallen to our generation to heal not only our own wounds, but also the wounds of our parents and our children.

While my book is one woman's perspective on what it means to persevere, I hope it inspires women and men alike to heal through claiming the power of their stories. In a work relevant to all generations, my memoir is one that belongs to every *person* faced with overcoming the odds of his or her upbringing—a reminder that we don't rise up in spite of our stories, we rise up *because* of them.

So I ask you to lean into your stories, embrace them, and share them. Know that we're not meant to stuff them away in our bodies—away from oxygen and light. Stories are powerful and therapeutic. Through mine, you will no doubt find parts of yours—so take what serves you.

May you find your redemption arc just as I have found mine; may you know on your journey that you are never alone.

Godspede, my friend.

CHAPTER 1

Dear Kwalimu

Dear Kwalimu,

It took your death, in January of 2020, for me to actually put pen to paper, the words pouring out of me when I did, to tell a story that is still unfurling.

It's true I had thought of fleshing the words out many times, but it wasn't until the 2020 coronavirus pandemic, the onset of which was marked by your death, that I began typing out Chapter One.

Yes, in the midst of my early work, I learned of *a sickness* that we would later come to find would catalyze worldwide trauma. No one knew the ins and outs of COVID-19 yet; it was still early in the year. But on January 29, as our family was walking out the door to celebrate Elijah's nineteenth birthday dinner, the phone rang. It was a call from our dear niece Rebekah, telling me that you passed away in your new home of California, far away from your motherland of Papua New Guinea. We were rocked and devastated by the news.

We all knew you'd been sick, but believed it was the flu, that it was certainly something you would survive. We had been praying for you... and just days before, you had posted a note to me on Facebook—"Loving You."

After the news of your death, still in a state of shock, Sarah Katherine and I made hasty arrangements to fly out to Half Moon Bay, San Francisco, where you lived. We were resolved to be there to retrieve your ashes on your birth family's behalf, given that the timeliness of their travel looked uncertain.

My brother Will was responsible for coordinating travel arrangements and handling communication between your family in Papua New Guinea and the coroner's office in California.

Sarah Katherine and I knew it would have to be a very quick trip for us, due to her school schedule and my work requirements. Prior to us leaving, my sister Steph contacted me, warning us to be careful during our trip as it was the location of many quarantined ships from California, due to the recent discovery of the virus from Wuhan. I had little knowledge of what she was talking about, even with my military background. *We just didn't know.*

After we arrived, we spent a sad but beautifully tender day and a half with your sister Boio and two other Papua New Guinea sisters, who had been able to come, after all, for your viewing and cremation. We left feeling relieved that Boio had been able to make the trip, given the constraints with distance and time.

Still in a state of acute grief, we flew back home to Texas on a Monday. By Wednesday, I was experiencing a strange tightness in my chest. I didn't give it much thought but attributed it to the flu that sent Elijah home from Austin College that same day, though I had been exposed to him after my symptoms began.

In the days that followed, I became very ill, losing my ability to breathe easily and feeling visited by a grim foreboding that settled in at night. I truly thought I was channeling your symptoms somehow —the knowingness of your suffering haunted me.

Kevin also fell ill with extreme symptoms, including fever, an unrelenting cough, weight loss, and difficulty breathing—especially while climbing the stairs. It wasn't until much later that we realized we'd contracted COVID-19. By then, there was adequate research on why Kevin had lost his sense of smell and taste.

Your suffering continued to haunt me, Kwalimu, even as I felt your presence all around. I knew you were the hawk that appeared, flying in the shape of an infinity sign over my house the day I arrived home. I also knew it was you who led me to notice the tiny wooden box marked "I love you"—with the earrings I gave you hanging on it—when I visited your home in Half Moon Bay.

You and I had always called ourselves *soul sisters*, and indeed, I felt your spirituality all around me, especially in the pain of missing you. In the months that followed, I knew that you had been called to lead the charge that humans were entering—a time that would be unlike any other, a time in which humankind would both suffer greatly and behave badly, while evolving more spiritually perhaps than in any other period of history.

• • •

It was during this season that a few close Dallas friends and I formed a group with the intention of reading Julia Cameron's *The Artist's Way* together. As you know from having lived in Taos, where the author herself lived, this book is quite the creative endeavor, loosely formatted around the twelve steps. By default, it mines up emotional blocks that keep us from accessing our best and highest selves. It takes courage and honesty to move through the process.

I had read it years before with another group of Dallas friends and experienced amazing results, and although I had been asked many times to join again, I felt it was such an emotionally large, life-changing experience that I could not envision repeating it. That was, until COVID-19.

Our group bonded quickly and formed a Facebook page to privately share within the group. Very early on, we were swapping stories that we had, in some cases, never shared before. Most, unsurprisingly, had to do with parents.

At the same time, I was working with a close friend who was getting certified to become a life coach. I had supported her by buying a few sessions from her and was jazzed by our meetings. At the end of my sessions, she suggested we continue to meet pro bono, as it was great educational fodder for her coaching. I agreed.

The stories that I shared with my group and my friend marked the first times I had ever broached the subject of certain events of my childhood, with many of them being extreme.

Likely my brother Peter shared with you many of our early family stories. As you know, since he was your husband, he certainly lived in an unedited, unapologetic way.

Not so much me, though—the youngest child, born ten years after Peter to a different father. In all of the circles I've been in, I've been an avid listener and processor of others' happenings but have rarely shared my own history. As a result, many made assumptions about who I was and where I came from, but, through no fault of their own, few had any inkling of the truth of my upbringing. I was very good at staying guarded.

When my mother took her life, it devastated all of us. Soon after, Steph moved away, and it was just my dad and us three youngest Pope children living at home.

As Peter may have shared with you, my father was a lone wolf, and while he did his best for all of us, we lived in extreme poverty and kept the world out. Most of the people that knew us didn't realize that we were living without a stove or refrigerator, that we had no heat or AC, or that we visited the pawnshop every week in order to have money for dinner. From the time my mother died and my older sister—who had been caring for us—moved away from home, we didn't have any guests in our house—until high school.

I can hardly think of that now. The effort required to be a walking fortress, a secret, having to maintain a separation between all that we were doing in the outside world and our home life, was huge and indescribable. It takes a lot to undo that once you become an adult.

Losing you, Kwalimu, was what woke me into realizing that I needed to live life 100 percent, expressing the truth of who I was for the first time, no longer keeping secrets. My sacred circle of girlfriends had also convinced me that my story needed to be heard, and that my message was valuable for others, no matter how difficult it was for me to tell it.

The messages I felt from you, Kwalimu—from the other side—made me certain that the time was *now*, and that leaving my job in order to pursue my true passions was an obvious decision. It was decided for me, without my being involved in the decision at all.

As divine coincidences go, the day after you passed, Sarah Katherine found a message you had written to Elijah and her. It was from one year prior and described a dream you had in which you were a distressed traveler, separated from your bags, and heading home.

In your dream, Sarah Katherine and Elijah were the ones who came through for you—to help you locate your belongings and make safe passage to your ultimate arrival to your family. This meant something to both of my children, whom you had been close to. You always loved children and trusted in the wisdom of young people —and your instincts in your life, and in your dream, still ring true: *It will always be the children who will help us find our way home.*

• • •

It's true that so much of my healing came after having my children. They've been the ones to show me the way home, back to my essential self. Through wanting to make the best world for them, they've helped me see clearly the ways in which our parents unwittingly wounded us—the generation of children raised in the '70s—and also the ways in which we created our own unique challenges for *their* generation.

This story of all of us has no real beginning and no end, but it's one in which we attempt to correct as the parenting pendulum swings by the decade.

Today I'm writing this book for Elijah and Sarah Katherine and for the work they will, no doubt, accomplish for themselves and for their babies. I write it in memory of my mother, a broken soul, and for all who walk through life a little bit fractured, feeling as though we haven't always had a seat at the table. This is for all of us who have felt the weight of our flaws and considered ourselves damaged, dysfunctional, and unworthy. It is for those of us who have kept secrets close, out of shame, feeling different, and not being like everybody else.

Welcome to the sisterhood and brotherhood of the beautifully broken. May you put your arms around your uniqueness and embrace the story of how you became wounded. May you learn to lovingly release the very thing that almost destroyed you, so that you can thank it for helping you become the stronger person that you are meant to be. And may that realization bring you all peace.

Yes, we're all broken in some way, and it makes us beautiful.

Kwalimu, thank you for showing me that there are, perhaps, no extraordinary people, only ordinary people who love and forgive others over and over again.

Poem for Kwalimu

Today we planned to gather,
My family and me,
To celebrate Kwalimu
Here in the Heart of Texas,
Old Granbury.

But the world had other plans
In the midst of this Corona (crown) -virus,

And yet in the midst of this Corona (crown) -virus,
We have found Corazona (heart) -virus.

And we are stopping, slowing down, loving each other,
Looking each other in the eyes.
Yes, in a God's eye view,
A movement came to the earth,
A movement divinely crown-guided,
That united all of us, the entire globe, in mere days.
And who was at the front of this movement?
This movement, divinely crown-guided
To love?
Someone very worthy.

Someone who had mastered love,
And people and friendship,
And being present.
Someone who would be an example
For others to refer to in their hearts
During their moments of learning.
To transform Corona into Corazona.

Thank you, Kwalimu.

I have heard it said that you are a champion of causes,
That you are everywhere like the wind.
You have been my most powerful of teachers,

And in loving myself and others,
I now see more clearly the yes's—and also the no's.

Yesterday, I sat with a wise circle of teens who said:
God always takes the good ones early.
And it struck me how beautiful it is that the good ones
are immortalized, made teachers and examples forever
through their passing, and we are thus led.

I felt Kwalimu tell me today,
"No regrets for the changed plans—
For in order for you to remember me, you must have forgotten me.
And that is not possible because I am in your hearts—
You need only breathe in to celebrate all that I am."

I heard her whisper to me,
"It is not necessary for you to remember me,
For you are living me,
All of you... in this new movement of the heart."
And so, I say to Kwalimu, we celebrate you forever.
Thank you for your courage in leading us all.
Thank you for your oh-so-sacred role in this spiritual
pilgrimage
That you have begun, and that we will finish—
As a people; as a world.
Love unto you, love unto us all,
Dear Kwalimu Kalypso Oceanrider.

Kalypso Kwalimu Harris, 2019 (photo credit to Susan Friedman)

CHAPTER 2

Dear Reader

Dear Reader,

> *"You are never alone, even during what you think are your weakest moments. You have thousands of years of powerful ancestors within you, the blood of the divine great ones in you, supreme intellect and royalty in you. Infinite strength is always on tap for you. Know that."*
>
> —UNKNOWN

I am the dream of my ancestors. I feel them all the time—reaching out, tugging on my spirit, telling me things with no words at all. I've heard these interactions referred to as *impressions*, and I have often wondered if I *impress* upon them from the natural realm. When they speak, I feel it physically. It begins in my center and radiates out, warmth spreading throughout me like thick honey. They communicate when I rest, when I pray, and when I create.

I have heard it suggested that Heaven connects to us on Earth through the pineal gland—known in Eastern thought as the crown chakra—where divine light illuminates us and shines through us to the outer world. In the same way, I consider myself an unfolding creation—a spiritual being, above time, walking out the ways of previous generations, as a conduit of reconciliation—hopeful to heal the trauma of the past with a present faith, confident the next generation will do the same for mine.

Perhaps it's what I said before: *our children will always show us the way home, show us the way to heal.* My children certainly do, and I find that, in the same way that they look to me as a model for their lives, I learn from them to grow past everything I've taught. We are not separate from those whom we cannot physically see; they learn through us as we redeem the past. I am the children of my ancestors; they look to me to help them, and they call out for me to take their hand and heal their wounds—so that their souls might finally have peace.

Recent studies—especially those in the field of somatic research—point toward epigenetics as a way to examine the inheritance of unhealed trauma. Stress can alter the material world through genetic inheritance, by turning particular genes on or off in our bodies—this is supported in works like *It Didn't Start with You* by Mark Wolynn,[1] who goes on to note that unhealed trauma can grow more pronounced with each generation, predisposing our children and their children to physical maladies and mental health issues.

From an evolutionary and sociological standpoint, it makes practical sense to heal our species by doing the necessary spiritual work required. But this doesn't always translate in Western society, where bookshelves are lined with answers to questions. As a result, we seem to feel more comfortable repeating than resolving with practical solutions. In my experience, the answer can be as simple as researching history, pulling out my paints, worshipping in song, or doing a quiet meditation. In a culture where everything is rapid, it can feel counterintuitive to pursue these activities with urgency, though they are often *mysteriously* the biggest influences on our physiological fitness.

The practice of slowing down helps us pace ourselves, teaches us stillness, and enables us to metabolize emotional trauma that can rise up unannounced, seemingly untethered to specific incidences. In our present reality, triggers present like a trip wire. They can be ours, or belong to someone beyond us—unexplainable fears from the consciousness of our ancestral lines that become embedded in our genes and psyche, playing on repeat until they are addressed and thereby physically put to rest.

I've lived enough life to understand there are plenty of people who are doubtful that our family still speaks to us from beyond, who are skeptical that we still store trauma from our past experiences. At one time, maybe I was doubtful as well—until I experienced it, and came to believe *that which you are seeking is causing you to seek.* Little did I know, I was being sought with regal demand.

In 2009, I began what would become a prolonged study on Henry VIII and his court. Over the years, I've read dozens of books on this topic, obsessively; many I've explored up to three times. While I was looking back at my Amazon purchases, a pattern revealed itself to me. Most of the works were by favorite author of mine, Philippa Gregory, who wrote about the English court. I'd read her work, pass it on, and then two years later I would unwittingly order the same book again. And again. And again.

Throughout my readings, I found that the happenings of court felt oddly familiar, as though I had been present somehow. I could imagine myself being there in a way that felt like a memory—while also experiencing an unrelenting physical and psychological heaviness that seemed to belong to me, but did not correlate to my individual circumstance. I would carry it with me, unsure of how to ask it to leave. My husband, Kevin, would sometimes joke, "Please, not another one…" as I'd pick up yet one more book on Henry VIII.

He knew that what I was reading would psychologically manifest in my present reality. That is, transported through time, I would feel personally the emotional betrayals of the past, being especially triggered by Henry VIII. Not only by the mistreatment and execution of his wives, but also by the chaos he stirred in his court by continually betraying his supporters—ultimately creating a dangerous, deadly game that rewarded loyalty with treachery.

One night, as I was reading about Anne Boleyn—Henry VIII's second wife, who was beheaded by his order—I was struck by a deep knowingness that I had emotional memories connected to her; we simply *must* be related. This realization was followed by a recognition that I felt I identified with *all* of the members of his court—whom I had come to know well through the many stories I'd absorbed. At that moment, I acknowledged that my notion was not so far-fetched. It made perfect sense that I might be in their collective lineage—as royalty married only royalty, they were all related to one another.

My premonition was confirmed in the summer of 2017. I was visiting the Farmers Market in Dallas, Texas, and encountered a stranger wearing a shirt with *Allred* printed on the front, which is my mother's maiden name. I approached him, then upon striking up a conversation, found that he and I were second cousins. Evidently, our grandfathers were brothers to Governor James V. Allred, who served in Texas from 1935 to 1939.

He shared that the Allred-Aldrich family line was related to Henry V of England. Having that connection as a lead compelled me to research our family tree and sure enough—Henry V was my fifteenth great-grandfather, making Henry VIII my second cousin fourteen times removed; William the Conqueror was my twenty-sixth great-grandfather, and Rollo the Viking my thirty-first great-grandfather. It's crazy to think that these prominent figures were in direct lineage with each other, but it's true. And the story of my ancestors doesn't stop there.

On the other side of my family line is William Bradford. I grew up knowing that he was our sixteenth great-grandfather on my father's side of the family. After doing thorough ancestry research, I came to find he was actually our tenth great-grandfather, which made me feel even closer to him.

As youngsters, my siblings and I heard a lot about Bradford at Thanksgiving. He was the governor of the Pilgrims who, against great odds, made the famous 1620 voyage aboard the *Mayflower* and founded Plymouth Colony. I always felt proud of my relation to him, and the part he played in our history—but there was something *else* there too. I felt a deep compassion for what he experienced—

his journey in choosing to leave England for the only future he could believe in. I imagined it was lonely, difficult, alienating, and heartbreaking. But he persevered, because something inside him made it a non-option to choose a lesser path.

Just recently, I watched *Desperate Crossing*,[2] a documentary on William Bradford and his journey on the *Mayflower*. Having not seen this specific piece before and not fully knowing his history, I cried at the depiction of a lonely twelve-year-old boy rifling through the Bible for comfort while enduring great sickness and the overwhelming loss of his family. As a youngster, Bradford felt disappointed in the adults around him, comparing their immoral behavior to the holy principles he was learning about in the gospel teachings. Because of this evident disparity, he felt convicted to leave England so that he could truly follow God. At the time of his decision, King Henry VIII's daughter Elizabeth was on the throne, which meant my mother's ancestors were in direct influence of my father's lineage.

It is not lost on me that generations ago, my mother's and my father's families lived in conflict with one another. The roles played out by King Henry VIII and William Bradford would eventually funnel down to the relationship between two turbulent lovers: Mom and Dad, who also lived with deep conviction, juxtaposing light and darkness, and whose demons I would be left to heal. Like William Bradford setting his sights on God as a child, I too chased miracles as a little girl—believing that I would arrive at the rainbow's end if I could muster my way through life's chaos. My journey, like Bradford's, taught me about the divine work of my heavenly father, *through* the mortal hands of my earthly Dad. Both were my *North Star*: my source of life, my truth, and my way out.[3]

William the Conqueror, my twenty-sixth great-grandfather, September 11, 2017, oil and pastel on canvas

My grandmother, Mary Slater Bradford,
eighth great-granddaughter of William Bradford

My daughter, Sarah Katherine, with my sister Mary and me, 2021.
It was windy at the tip of Cape Cod where the Pilgrims first landed and thrilling to finally stand there. One day soon I will return with my son, Elijah Kevin Bradford Sisk, namesake of his Pilgrim forefather.

CHAPTER 3

Dear Mama

Dear Mama,

Most of my memories are mine, but they are not mine. All are either permeated with your presence or stained with your absence. I miss you. I have always missed you, even when you were alive. There were too many of us—ten ruckus siblings packed into the house at Benbrook Boulevard, and only three of us were Popes, with Dad's last name. You'd been married three times before your plan to have the hysterectomy that would lead to the discovery that you were pregnant—*with me*, the baby. Perhaps that was the closest any of us ever were to you—tucked away in your womb, among the haunt of your deepest griefs.

Dad, in his wisdom, sensed early on what science now considers a link between gynecologic and mental health. Your hysterectomy proved to be your undoing, and this is true for many women of the era who struggled to maintain their sanity after surgery. The hormonal fluctuations paired with the chemical imbalance of depression positioned you for immense suffering.[4]

You'd smoked during pregnancy with all of us, alternating between addictions. When it wasn't the high of oxytocin from having babies, it was nicotine. The smoke from the glowing end of your cigarettes would dance up into the night—eerie, mystical, and translucent, like the ghost you would be to all of us as we got older, and to the men who had loved you, including Dad.

I wonder if our desire for you tore at you the way it would tear at me to see Elijah and Sarah Katherine not getting enough from me. I cannot imagine what it would have been like for you, with five daughters and five sons, to feel that you don't have enough energy to match the love you need to express, or how your psyche must have suffered in your decline, in the forever moments of tiredness, anger, guilt, sadness, disappointment, and frustration. There was no time to sort out your mental health, no space to take a breath, no escape for proper clarity.

Amid the cacophony and clutter of endless dishes, laundry, loud fighting, and snarly dogs, amid the coming and going of swaths of friends and strangers in our home, there was no moment of silence for you to hear your own voice. The low, critical voice of your mother eclipsed everything; it paired with the ambient sound of a love you could never find in her, as you dragged your own little-girl self behind you, never stopping to examine your wounds—a love so vaporous, it could not be caught, or distilled in a jar.

Even in the face of the disappointment regarding your mother, you preserved your countenance, never acknowledging that it was your only sense of protection against bringing shame upon the family.

Your uncle was the governor of Texas; he stood regal, professional, and esteemed. As the daughter of his brother, who was also a prominent lawyer and businessman, it meant something that you were an artist who had made a significant mark on the community, and thus upheld the family legacy through your great mind.

However, your artistic accomplishments could not compensate for the disappointment you brought on the Allred name by having not one, not two, but three husbands, and for bringing more babies into the world than was practical. Each child was a growing liability to your parents. They tried to help, first by hiring Beatrice, and then by buying the Taos Land, but neither served to bring the stability they'd hoped to introduce.

With almost a PhD, you worked as an English professor, then established your foundation in the theater and had your name printed in the playbills of the children's musicals you'd written and produced. You were hired as the head of the children's theater for Casa Mañana, an esteemed position, and created Ideas in Motion, a Montessori school complete with a school board, in the basement of the famed Scott Theatre in Fort Worth. There, little ones could feel paint between their fingers and experience freedom as they learned—a freedom you craved in your own life.

You even developed the popular cooking show *Bon Vivant*. Your accomplishments were astounding, especially for a woman with so many children—the *right* people saw that. Everyone who loved you was taken by your unbridled creativity and your devotion to the growth of the community, even at the expense of yourself, and by default—us.

In the 1960s, there was little emphasis on self-care, mental health, and marital healing. You'd bargain for hours from the day and come up with nothing. Your beloved writing always came at the cost of your own sleep, something that would erode your mental health over time—beyond the diagnosis they gave you of being *manic depressive.*

In the 1960s, society was making strides to deinstitutionalize mental health care. This was intended as a positive change, but doing away with asylums collapsed the infrastructure. Mental health professionals were beginning to emerge but were not yet established in the hospitals—where cases like yours were moving—so many fell through the cracks. Though they were also trying to destigmatize mental illness, it had historically been considered a spiritual issue: demonic possession, darkness, something that needed to be cast out by a spiritual leader. As a result, there was no safe space to talk about your issues; there was no one who would understand.

Back then, hysterectomies were a common practice, with no true medical consideration given to the extremeness of the procedure or the possible negative consequences. Dad knew better, knew right away that yours was a terrible mistake and anguished as he watched your mental health decline. When they stitched you up, I wonder if you felt yourself slipping away.[5] By the time they'd put you on lithium, you were a ghost of yourself, and worse, when they took you off of it abruptly, the doctors all but ensured your subsequent suicide attempts. Afterward, you were admitted to a mental hospital, where you were prescribed electric shock treatments, which claimed what remained of you.[6]

When you were sent to the mental hospital, your visits with us stopped entirely, making us more heartsick for you than ever before. Your brain was restless and progressive, probably a threat—your greatest asset and worst enemy, something you were conditioned to feel ashamed of and desperately longed to tame.

You left a wound that never healed in the family; the reopening of it continued year after year. Though I have surpassed you in age, the extreme rawness of it has only just recently begun to subside. I remained a little girl in many ways until I turned fifty.

Until finally, I was big enough, brave enough, to admit to my circle of friends how much it hurt to lose you—to have had you only for a scarce few precious years.

As a child, your death was far worse than dying myself. It was as if the sun fell from the sky. There was no light. No heat. No day. Just cold, dirty floors. And Dad, whose only star had burned out, drove himself more intensely than ever, seeking to bleed off the pain through exhausting himself, physically working until the mind would turn off and the body would shut down, so that sleep could finally come. And nothing ever felt right again.

Your own pain was palpable up until the last days you spent with us. I could feel it in the fighting, while listening to you and Dad argue a lot. I lived for the peace in between, and I wanted those moments to last forever. I loved you both. I wanted you to get along. But even then, I sensed the fight beyond the fight, the pain beneath the pain. Your points were complex, cryptic, and non-relatable. I could feel you two not loving each other. And I felt scared.

Put up the food for once in your life! the note you left read. I watched Dad crumple it up in his hands, then study it for a long time. I could feel him grieving the familiar, inevitable cycle of you lashing out aggressively. The more erratic your behavior became, the more he carried the heartache of losing someone he loved to mental illness. I remember looking around at the empty kitchen, which had been vibrant in other years, now neglected. It was a hallmark of time passing, a symbol of the nourishment we received, or didn't, year in and year out.

I wasn't sure where our food was stored. I wondered if it was hidden away behind the oven door, cooking, like one of those families on television, or if we put it away differently. *I knew we were different*—your mental illness kept us isolated. It was a secret that had been imposed upon all of us. It was not socially acceptable to address—by anyone. No one was willing to understand the correlation between depression, hormone imbalance, and mental health . . . because that belief might contradict the immediate supposition that a person struggling with such issues was *flawed*.

You moved away, to the mental hospital, and became abstract in my mind. Every now and then you'd return—ethereal, like the magic of midnight striking in a fairy tale, surreal enough to not entirely believe. My whole body would freeze when I'd first see you again, so craving your hug, yet there was so much at stake. We would make our way to you, slowly at first, not sure entirely if we could trust in the moment, in you being there, in you staying, but ready to give ourselves fully. Sometimes I held back, longer than the others, praying, then knowing that you'd make your way to me. As the baby, I was your special one.

You would sleep with me, snuggling. I would breathe the smell of you deeply, to make a memory, in case you left for good next time and never came back. The feeling of you leaving the bed was torturous. I was never sure if you would return. When you were there, you were everything I wanted. When you were gone, there was only emptiness, and it overtook my every waking thought.

You taught me how to play opossum, and not the scary kind that would later haunt my childhood, but to pretend I was sleeping when Dad would call from the other room. To steal more moments with me, you'd say, "Pretend you don't hear him."

He'd continue to call my name, and as much as I didn't want to ignore him, I felt I had no choice; if I didn't listen, I thought you'd go away again. So I'd lay there, pretending to be asleep. Those moments were awful—the moments in which being with you was ruined because the price of your love was for me to hurt Dad.

Once, before you'd been hospitalized, you were wild-eyed and enraged. In a frenzy, you dumped all of the garbage in the house into the front seat of Dad's station wagon. You asked us to help you, expecting that we would, insisting that *he deserved it.*

So I lingered nearby, pretending to help, silently praying under my breath to God and to Dad to not be upset. I was appalled that you would make such a mess on purpose. The house was always suffering and needed so much. These episodes made me feel like we were working against ourselves—regressing, when we were already so many steps behind.

But, as bad as the fighting was, it became worse when you were put in the mental hospital. After you regained your orientation from the trauma of shock therapy, you wrote us letters. I have no idea how long this went on, nor was I ever fully able to respond, until now.

• • •

Dad made the tough decision to divorce you after two similar accounts of neglect. The first was after I swallowed roach poison as a baby. I'd been looking for something in the cabinets, under the sink, unsupervised. The second was after he found me, as a toddler, asleep on the kitchen floor, soaked in my own tears. I'd been looking *for you.*

He knew that if your unintentional abandonment did not stop, he'd lose custody of his own three children—and quite possibly the Harris children that he'd taken on from your second marriage, but never formally adopted. There could be no more leaving us in strange places, like street benches, or inviting me to sleep beside you and Straw Man, the lover you took in the throes of your mental illness, while you were still committed to Dad.

The decisions you made in your state of insanity killed you, killed him—killed all of us; they echoed through the hallways at Benbrook, as the shadow of *the love that could have been* haunted us.

Dad loved all of you, with all that he had. It was not his wish to separate from you, to have you depart us to live with your oldest daughter, Patricia—who was twenty-one years older than me, and sisterly enough for me to understand she belonged to us, but who inevitably felt like a stranger. You moved all the way to Maryland, and your letters continued, except they were from a new address.

I would always feel wonder at how you found a way to insert a pure chocolate lollipop into the envelope of each message, and astonishment that they were never *entirely* melted. They were delicious, and I'd eat my chocolate sucker while also devouring your words, straining to remember the sound of your voice.

Every time I got one of your letters in the mail, I would retreat to our dirty living room, where it was cool, and sit on the old, dilapidated couch and feel, for a few moments anyway, that all was right with the world. I could read how much you loved me, sensing the intentionality in choosing a beautiful, magical, chocolate sucker just for me—in full consideration of my little-girl self and what I needed. Holding your letter would bridge the distance between us—just for a few moments, you were present again, making me sure of your love.

Despite all the painful years of conflict, Dad never spoke ill of you behind your back, no matter how brokenhearted, no matter how devastated. He knew, decades before the doctors did, that the hysterectomy was your undoing, that the lithium prescription and its rapid withdrawal sealed your fate. And so, he only spoke well of you and always with hope for your healing.

He'd driven the three Pope siblings to the park that day, then got down on one knee. He said he had something important to tell us. I was confused because his mannerisms were off in a way I'd never seen. One moment later his head dropped into his hands and his whole body shook. At first, I confused it with laughter. Until our eyes met.

"I have something very sad to say," he began. "I got a call from your sister Patricia. Your mother went to sleep this morning and never woke up."

We stood quiet, all around him, little sheep gathering near a trusted shepherd, instinctively circling to protect him as well. It didn't make sense. The words were too large to process. I stared into his face, searching his eyes, trying to comprehend, in my five-year-old mind, that I would never see you again.

You'd died of an overdose. The emergency room couldn't save you in the end, nor could the doctors—couldn't call back your soul this time, even though they had before. This time they couldn't beckon you back into your body.

As an adult I learned that you screamed in pain as you were dying, pleading to God and the angels to undo your choice to leave us. Later that year, I'd find in a letter to Dad the words, *I can't be without my baby Phoebe anymore.* That made me certain, at age six, that I'd somehow caused your death.

It would be many years until I was able to accept that you were actually gone—more *gone* than you had been before. Mary said I used to cry myself to sleep every night. I don't remember that. But I do remember playing pretend. In my imagination, I could always have you with me, coming to pick me up from school, where I could be proud that *I too* had a mother who loved me so much that she was coming to get me early from school. I turned ten before I accepted you were never coming back.

No, I couldn't have possibly known any of this in the moment that Dad told me that you'd died. My tears that morning, at Bellaire Park in Fort Worth, were scant, and more in support of Dad than anything, because there was no way to grasp the totality of how my world had changed forever.

When Dad scooped me up in his arms, and walked us three young Popes down to the creek at the park, I showed delight to him as he pointed out the colored aquarium rocks that someone had dumped in the creek water. I gave my best to him, in the saddest moment of our lives, because I could see he only ever wanted us to be happy. We celebrated the colored rocks. They did seem magical.

After you died, he only ever praised you—to the ten of us, and to other adults. We children never spoke about you because the pain was so big, we had to walk around it. The adults didn't bring it up, because they didn't want to make us sad. No one needed a household of grieving children on their hands, or to further burden a broken father who was already carrying the weight of the world.

That's a lot of years of not talking about you, Mama, a whole lot of years of loving and missing you so much, it swallowed us up and made us turn our sadness inward. I learned not to tell, not to talk, not to explain, because then I would cry and the world would know. It's like when you died, that sadness inside you turned to dust that settled in our lungs. It was hard to breathe, but we had to figure out a way somehow. We could never cough up enough of it to live carefree again, to experience ease. It was always inside the crawlspace of our ribcages—where we kept all the family secrets.

After you died, no one was allowed in the house. We locked out the sky, the seasons, the trees, and all the friends we could have had. Our hearts were closed; we only had the Benbrook Boulevard house, which I never believed could feel emptier until you were gone.

Being loved by you made me whole in a way nothing else ever did. I can still feel the brush of your cheek against mine, even back to infancy—where I must have known it was important to catch you like a miraculous firefly in a jar, holding my breath, watching you flicker until finally you dimmed to nothingness.

Your potential was endless, as was our potential together; to catch a tiny glimpse of what could have been still makes me want to chase a hope that isn't here. I can't bring you back to life outside of the part of you that lives in me, the part of you that shows up when I ignite my own children.

I tried to honor your memory by becoming only your good parts. I never wanted to hurt people, take my life, or drive myself crazy in the name of creativity, which I have found to be a sacred, holy act. Creating brought me to life in the years when I needed you most, and especially around age nine, when I was visibly broken, with my long, shaggy hair, jeans that grazed the pavement, and clothes that would keep me concealed entirely—so that I would be divorced from femininity, and daughterhood, divorced from the reality of having been yours.

As a young teen, I kept you at arm's length. I spoke about you by your name, in third person, and remained detached from my feelings by using clinical terms only, so that no one would suspect for a second the pain I had been through. To speak of you, even a little, in real ways would have been to publicly invite the entirety of my pain. I simply could not.

Throughout my adult life, I've been careful about maintaining my diet and what I put in my body as a way to control my emotions and my mental state at all times—to shield myself from flaky, unreliable, unpredictable, and irrational behaviors because I feared I might cause others pain. Inadvertently, I shielded myself from being fun-loving and carefree as well. Because relaxing and enjoying, somehow, might lead to indulgence and irresponsibility. I could not, would not, risk taking flight in the way that you did, destroying myself, destroying others.

On a recent Mother's Day, I found a portrait of you that I had painted years ago. I looked into your eyes and knew that I was very much like you, as a mother and as a woman, and that I was glad for this. I accepted everything you were, and everything you were not. Your talents. Your beauty. Your vulnerability. Your mystery. And I loved you, just as much as I had when I was little and you were captivating.

That was the pivotal moment in which I realized not only that I was like you, but also that I was proud to be like you—proud to be your daughter. In the way your spirit still lives inside of me, God is inside of me—neither intangible nor far away. And from that moment forward, I realized I will never, ever again have to search for either of you.

My goal in life is to love big, like both you and the Creator. I am proud of you, for your maternalism, creativity, expansiveness, and exuberance, for your ability to bring all the wonder into our tiny world. You reached up and selected all the stars from Heaven and brought them down to us. Though at times you felt too ethereal to ever touch, we got to love you, and we felt lucky, even if it was only from afar. I can offer that to my children up close. I can grant them the wishes you did not have the strength left to fulfill.

Out of everyone who made their way throughout our house—the noisemakers, the artists, the turbulent, and the soft, I have grown to accept that I am the most like you. And, like you, I have parts of me that are vulnerable, emotions that are too big for the moment, times when I feel I must draw the curtains on the world to renew myself.

Kevin understands. We've come from different families, different places, but he also knows what it means to have emotions that are too big. Still, we both keep showing up for each other, we understand that we are still parenting the children within us, we know that neither one of us is leaving. We're both a little wild in spirit; we wait for the other, even when we mess up or misbehave. I chose someone who cares for me the way Dad cared for you, even through the divorce. He loved one woman his whole life: you, Mama. And as the mama in my home, I hold space and demonstrate forgiveness, for the times when things are too big, when emotions are too heavy to keep it all in check.

You are timeless, Mama, and you are ever awake in the creative choices that I make moment-to-moment, in my writing, in my life reflections, and in the way I love my children. You are alive in my memories, most of which are mine, but not entirely mine—and all of them are *you*.

Phoebe's portrait of Mama, 2017

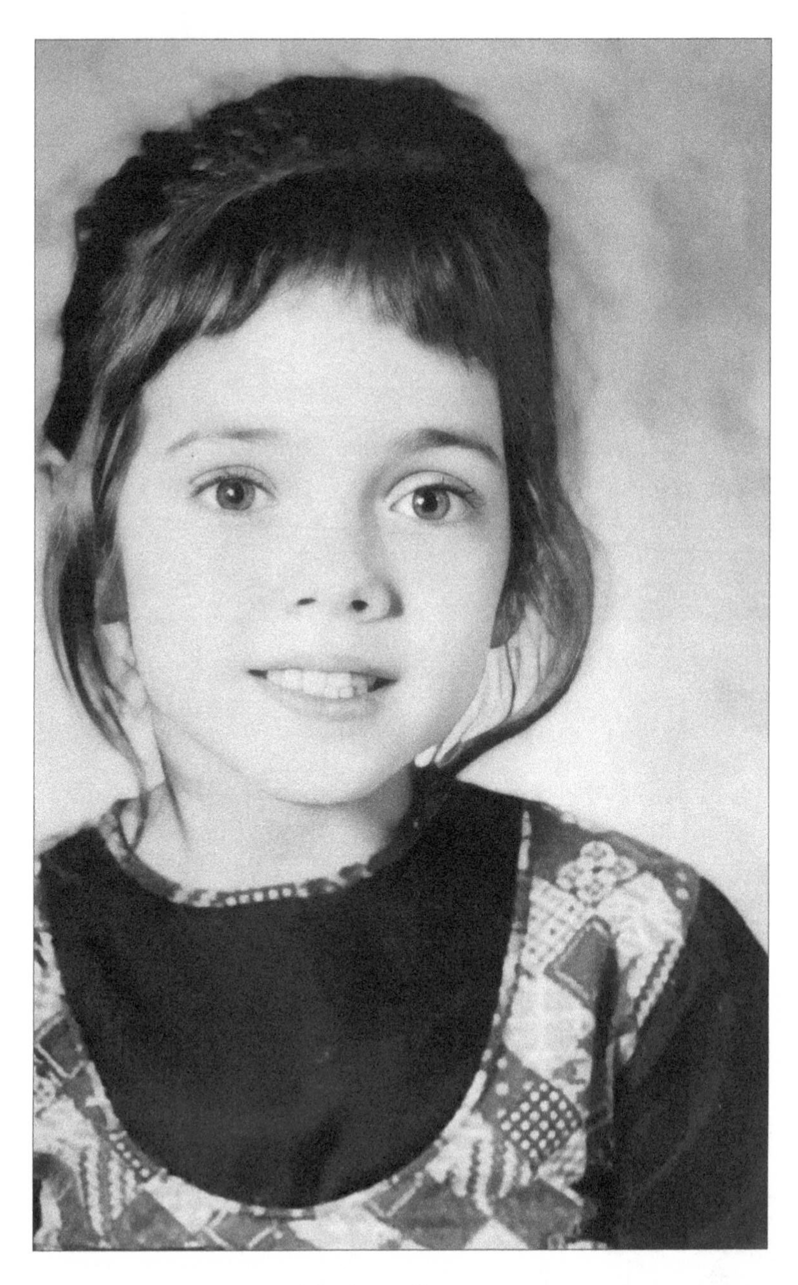

Phoebe, age five, 1972

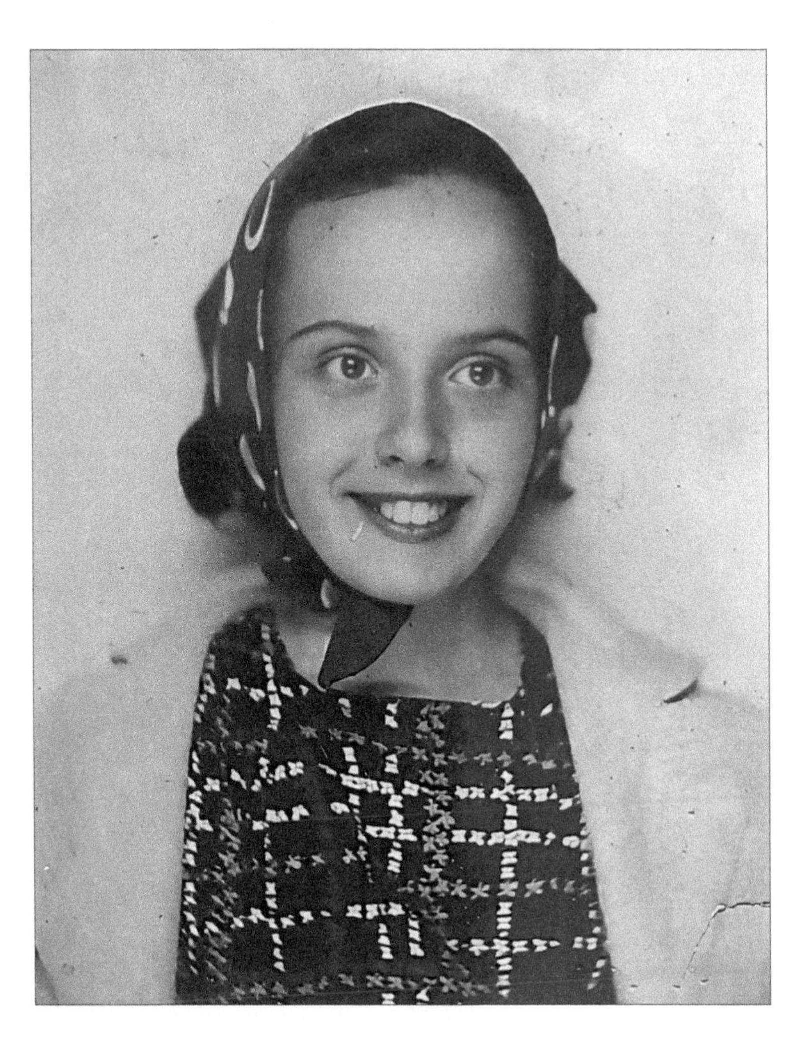

Mama, age twelve, 1940

CHAPTER 4

Dear House at Benbrook Boulevard

Dear House at Benbrook Boulevard,

Your walls were wrought with blood and secrets. You framed dark corners, naked mattresses on the floor, children who raised themselves, and scuttling creeping things. The heart and solace of you was in Dad's embrace, when he'd pick up the pieces *again*. I never meant to get into the roach poison—the reason their marriage ended, the last of too many reckless nights endangered by Mama's mania, after her surgery and decline, while Dad strived to keep the house together.

Mama. I cried for her, alone in the dark on the dirty, linoleum floor. My cheeks were raw from tears. In the other room, I could hear the thumping of tails and dog paws scratching. Shawna's scruffy mutt body overpowered me, while chubby dachshund Greta paid me little attention in her daily routine, as I was not an alpha and therefore of no use to her. I was in awe of them, and a little scared of them, too, because once when they littered at the same time, they stole pups from each other and killed them.

Shawna was dominant and chose the sock drawer at the foot of the stairs as a place to birth and nurse her pups. But even the tall sides did not keep Greta from scaling them to retaliate once the pup stealing began. It seemed unbelievable to me that they would do that, and needless to say I was horrified to witness their tiny babies' limp, innocent bodies snatched so viciously.

And the anguish didn't stop there. When the mother dog returned to find a pup missing, she would worry frantically, whining and searching the area.

Steph found the first pup, killed by Shawna, and I spotted the second, killed by Greta, dead under the bed next to a spot of blood. I wondered why no one saw it or cleaned it up and then realized it was because no one knew.

I happened to be there when Steph hung her head off the bed upside down, playing around, then spotted it and screamed. I had already known about it lying there for a full day; I just didn't know how to process it. I remember thinking how different the pups looked, one a true tiny mutt and the other a dachshund, and realized that it didn't matter. It didn't change how equally horrifying it was to witness them both.

We were in close quarters, but it often felt like we could not keep up with each other. We were so many people circulating through a house, meeting various needs, at different ages, coming and going, with no resting point and no mutual connection time.

I was loved a lot... as *the baby*—picked up and hugged by everyone. But I'd decided, maybe in the womb, that I would be born into the world and make my way out of our family quickly. Not because I didn't love them, but because I loved all of us too much to continue witnessing the cruel inevitability of a winner and a loser in the ongoing competition for scarce resources, like the vicious rivalry played out by our mother dogs.

I couldn't shoulder the emptiness that we all endured, even in a house full of other children. We were a byproduct of her—a mess hall of kids, all with clanking trays, all with hungry hearts for her love. But there was only one *Mama* being pulled in every direction.

There were ten of us—two Masons, five Harrises, and Three Popes. I was the last Pope—*Phoebe*, Mama's favorite by virtue of me being *the baby*.

Patricia Mason, *Patty*, was the oldest; she was justice-minded, a dancer, and a philosophical protester in the '70s. She'd later grow up to also almost earn her PhD in mental health counseling.

Patty was close and loyal to Mama, being that she was a true intellectual and private about personal matters. She had the clearest eyes of the lightest blue and mostly wore her hair fashionably short, being physically robust and sturdy throughout her life. It was perhaps Mama's death that was part of the reason she chose to discontinue dancing—something she'd always loved.

Afterward, she carried the sensitivity of burying a dream wherever she went, often broaching the subject to just as quickly justify that her knees had made her quit.

Patty was a talented writer, and she was artful in composing songs. She raised three kids with similar passions and gifts. She and my mother got pregnant and gave birth in tandem—my mother at thirty-seven, with the Pope twins, and Patricia at twenty, with

Jennifer. They would repeat this cycle sixteen months later, when Mama had me and Patricia had Aaron. Patricia's husband's name was David Gilmartin. They were attracted to each other's minds and philosophies, and made for a beautiful couple that could value the complexity of life.

Johnny Mason was baby number two. He was childlike, perhaps even more so as he grew older, and carried himself in the knowledge that he was loved by his mother, who adored him for his like sensibilities with music and theater. During the years that I knew him, he was docile—gifted with sensitivity and innocence. He was a master of the banjo, living much of his life as a performing musician in Taos, New Mexico, where he enjoyed lasting friendships and produced several CDs. Often Johnny would appear unattached to reality, but simultaneously could show an uncanny ability to tap into a *knowingness* that transcended the senses.

One night, in high school, I went running alone very late at night, to Mama Harris's house—mother of Joe Harris, and honorary grandmother to us all. When I arrived, he was outside. He told me that he'd been waiting for me, which was odd, because I'd only made my spontaneous decision twenty minutes earlier. He offered to run with me, so we jogged off into the night—barely speaking a word through the entire experience. Somehow, we didn't need to.

Johnny and I shared a penchant for finding God most everywhere. We both came to know that it was a good, necessary thing. In our later years, we prayed frequently together.

Johnny had hazel eyes and a peculiar hair color—in fact, I'm still unable to describe the hue resulting from its mix of blond, red, and green undertones. As I knew him, Johnny wasn't necessarily a physical sort of person, but he was attentive to his looks—choosing pants and dressier shirts, never shorts or a T-shirt. He always presented himself neatly, without appearing to give it any thought at all.

Kate Harris was baby number three. She was the quintessential flower child of the family and her friend circle, and she looked it —bearing a small frame; masses of kinky, curly dark hair with a sometimes headband; and piercing blue eyes. She wore jeans, cutoff shorts, and T-shirts almost exclusively and was a rabid fan of the Beatles, even winning free tickets as a teen to see them live. That was Kate—ever in the middle of the most exciting circles, being perceived as both carefree and more than a little lucky. She had lots of friends and drove the party wagon in high school—a VW bus—and no doubt they all smoked their share of pot inside.

She was a vivacious, funny, social leader, always up for a good time. She was talented at sewing and would design her own clothing, which came in handy when she became a young mother, like Mama and Patricia, at age seventeen. Kate would go on to have seven kids total—three boys and four girls from three different fathers, just like Mama.

Jody Harris was Mama's fourth, and the oldest Harris brother. He was loving and smiled a lot, perhaps because he lacked confidence, through no fault of his own. Whatever the reason, his smile and sweetness never disappointed in drawing in others, transcending the moment to higher possibilities. Heartbreakingly, in his teenage years, he sometimes seemed to invite being labeled as lazy and unintelligent by adults, though he was neither. He had a big mind and an even bigger heart, showing, quite likely, the greatest emotional intelligence of the family in the ways that he cared for us little ones. He loved resting in the cool living room on a hot Texas summer day, reclining on the couch while eating peanut butter toast. The best part was that he always had the kindness, awareness, and wherewithal to make a slice for us Pope kids as well.

Jody was fascinated by black holes in outer space. Not surprisingly, they became his passion and remained so into adulthood, and it was then that we understood the true depths of his intelligence. His appearance was downright charming, being possessed of blue eyes, curly hair, and an artful gap between his teeth. In fact, he charmed a young, beautiful girl named Nancy into marrying him, and they set their hardworking habits early by buying a house together. Jody cared about responsibility and helping others, so fittingly, he joined the Navy and became a dental hygienist, returning later to invite us Three Popes around the bathroom sink to show us how to properly brush our teeth. He became a father young and raised two kids who were both intelligent and creative thinkers.

Stephanie Harris was child number five in the birth order, and came out with her own looks that seemed to belong to no one else in the family. She was elfish and immensely cute—with blonde hair, green eyes, and a big, beautiful toothy smile. Like Kate, she was tiny, not much over 5' 3", with a little frame.

Steph came into the world ready to mother—and once Mama passed, she mothered all of us through cooking, cleaning, baking cookies, and getting us young ones ready for school. She was artful in all that she did, so when she fixed our hair and dressed us, we looked very cared for and ready for the day, whether or not we felt it. Clothes were another palette for Steph, and she was adept at pairing unique colors and textures—a mustard yellow, velvet shirt with green corduroy overalls; an A-line dress with just the right finishes, and black patent shoes to match. Steph would cut our hair as well—creating just the right amount of bangs, and arranging tendrils of hair to frame our faces. It was always a mystery where she had learned to do such things.

Steph was consistently sensitive, deliberate, and responsible—the older sister who reached down to help us younger ones. She had the Midas touch in the household, so that everything she touched became art, leaving beauty in her wake, her work never done. As a teenager, Steph paid close attention to our wounds and even as an adult, she still nurses mine. She carries the awareness of the universe and the bravery to walk an individual path—both her spirit and her presence are complete—and there are no stones left unturned in conversations with her.

Steph also became a young mother, losing one in the hospital by herself at seventeen years old; this was followed shortly thereafter by the birth of Sam, who gave her both purpose and beauty. She had four kids—three boys and one girl, Matty, who was born in New York in the back of Steph's Volvo, so they aired the birthing story on *Good Morning America.*

Peter Harris was baby number six, the third boy in the family, who had the darkest of hair and green eyes. The intensity of his looks could match his keen sense of humor and also the sarcasm he sometimes showed, probably from being let down one too many times—or worse, in a few big, important ways.

We often suspected that somehow Peter got the brunt of the *worst of it*, from his father Joe Harris, before he came to live with us at Benbrook Boulevard.

It seemed to be true, because although he often made himself more present than the others, and extended support in unexpected ways, he was also capable of retracting whatever goodness he had offered at the first hint that it might not be reciprocated. So certain were his expectations of people failing him that they would sometimes become a self-fulfilling prophecy. It always seemed heartbreaking, somehow, as an observer to this.

It wasn't until I witnessed his act of brutality with the opossums that I realized how deeply he must have suffered at the hands of his father. They'd snuck under the house, into Dad's unfinished bathroom, and did not fare well once Peter brought out his bat.

Peter was exceptional with both tools and humor—possessing a quick and fiery wit and excelling at building, carpentry, and living off the land. As an adult, he carried his skills into a maintenance profession, and ended up in management at one of the big Taos ski resorts, working alongside his beloved and spirited wife, Kwalimu, who succeeded in creating a homegrown culture of hospitality for the hotel. While it's true that Peter, no doubt, lived the darkest of what his father, Joe Harris, offered to his children, it's also true that he attracted the brightest light in his world for many, many years through his marriage to Kwalimu. In those years, as any good spouse is capable of, they made each other both beautiful and whole.

Ben Harris was the vulnerable, pure-hearted brother. He grappled with existential dilemmas such as the inherent duality of the nature of man—the fact that we, as a people, were capable of goodness but also programmed for suffering. He grieved humanity. His spirit baptized us all.

He was living in the house with Patricia when Mama took her life, and it affected him mightily. Afterward, he returned to Fort Worth to live with his father, Joe, and stepmother, Jimmy, and attended Paschal High School, as did all the children in our family.

Ben was a straight-A student and earned a four-year scholarship to TCU—where Mama went. All the girls who knew him had a crush on Ben, but he was in love with Janet, his high school sweetheart and fellow class favorite. He had beautiful brown hair and deep brown eyes. Sweet, intelligent, aware, and respectful he was—yet he could tease mercilessly when he so chose.

He was certainly one of the overachievers of the family. He excelled during the hardest years of all—high school—holding a steady management position at the local Baskin-Robbins and planning for a future that seemed bright.

That was, until early in his college years when Janet called to break up with him. She was attending BYU—a Mormon college in Utah. She claimed that the church had always been there for her, yet Ben had only known her during her teen years, so she was less trusting of their relationship. Ben was devastated. So he, the non-drinker and non-drug taker of our family, consumed multiple hits of purple microdot acid in an attempt to leave this world.

Instead of departing to the other side, he compromised his sanity permanently and never earned the degree he set out to achieve. His condition was worsened by the psychotropic drugs he was prescribed after overdosing. Watching Ben go in that way was far worse than losing him to death.

As a youngster, Ben had struggled with sadness. He had temper tantrums, due in part to Peter's antagonism, and was somehow lost in the chasm between the Harrises and Popes.

After overdosing, he started hearing voices that would erode his reality over time. This led to his diagnosis of schizophrenia, which meant more medicines, more side effects, and more departure from reality.

He lived and died in Taos—not on the family land, but in the government housing that was part of his disability pension. Within months after Jody passed at age sixty due to liver disease, Ben lost his will to live. He succumbed to the shadows of his own mind and surrendered his life to a recreational drug overdose seven months later. Right after Jody died, there was an enormous breakthrough in black holes that made national headlines. I had a sense it was Jody, uncovering the mystery from the other side, and letting us all in on the secrets he'd been dying to discover.

The first Pope was Abigail. She never made it into this world due to "complications" with the pregnancy. The doctors believed it was due to the domestic violence Mama endured at the hand of her second husband, Joe Harris, as punishment for falling in love with Dad. After a blow to Mama's stomach, Abigail's tiny body hemorrhaged —so our oldest tiny Pope went back to God. She hovers here, and I know her in spirit, just as familiarly as William and Mary.

And then there was us, The Three Popes. Mary and William Pope were twins—Mama's only pair. Being my biological sister, and older only by sixteen months, Mary was my closest friend growing up. In the years when Mama became more of a figment of my memory than something real, Mary reminded me what it felt like to come home.

Mary was good and always sweet and neither of us seemed capable of misbehaving much—always wanting to do the right thing, to listen and comply. In our elementary and middle school years, even though we'd spent all day together in the classroom, we often sat at the dining room table and played games or wrote notes to each other.

William was a mighty cute boy, albeit full of mischief, in part because his quick mind would look to entertain itself when bored. He was inherently very good in nature, but often owned the label—thrown out by adults being irresponsible with their language—of being *bad* when his mischievous side took over.

In his formative years, he began to believe it. Being the youngest male Pope was sometimes painful for William as the extended Pope family unwittingly favored us girls, due to the strong Wheeler women in our family on my father's side who, I learned years later, treated men as second-class citizens. This culture—right or wrong—formed in the family and was passed down, leaving Will to often feel isolated.

Though Will teased Mary and me mercilessly, we were still allies. We'd walk home together after school, carrying all of our books and our clarinets too. The fact is that we Popes clung tight to our studies and school achievements as the house around us was falling down.

We were in all of the honor societies, including the one for Spanish students. We played in the marching band and wrote for the school newspaper. There was strength in our trio; we were a united front against the world.

Benbrook House, you enveloped us all. And we tried our best to take care of you. When Dad was away working at the zoo, Ben would come to visit and help us try to set the kitchen right again, after years of it being neglected. Later, Dad taught us how to cook, wash dishes, and keep the sink wiped down in between tasks.

Benbrook House, do you remember, years earlier, when Ben got his dad, Joe Harris, to drop him off at our house on Thursdays so that we could have playtime together? He wanted to be there for us. I wonder where he learned such a thing when it really wasn't modeled for him? Or was it? Maybe the one thing all of us kids learned was to do our best to take care of the young and the innocent. Maybe you witnessed that on behalf of all of us.

On one visit, Ben expressed anger that we'd gotten into his things that were packed away upstairs after he had moved out. We Three Popes had left them alone for months, but one day, a tiny knife caught our eye, and we couldn't resist opening the boxes. We felt terrible in the moment that he chastised us for this, especially because we could see the grief in Ben's eyes.

It hurt him immensely to be caught in between families. Although we weren't raised in church, and Dad held his own skepticisms about God, Ben seemed to know early on about our Creator. He sensed God was something magnificent that should have brought him relief but only seemed to make his time here, separate from the divine, hurt all the more.

Once, we Three Popes celebrated Christmas with him. The three of us chipped in to buy him a St. Christopher medal, which he really wanted. He was delighted to open it, then returned to the tree saying, "Okay, time to get another present for everyone, and one for Ben too!" He was referring to himself. When he looked under the tree, we three children fell silent—there was no other present for Ben, and we knew it. There was not enough money. It was always hard for the kids in our family on this side of Heaven, especially after Mama left us.

Sometimes, I would ask Dad about God, and he would say, "God is an idea." He never seemed to care too much about what people thought of him—except, as we got older and the Baptists crucified him for not coming to church, I could tell he began to wonder about an afterlife. Hopefully he felt Mama as his angel after she left this earth, but Dad didn't have much to sing praises about, except us kids, whom he loved enough to keep surviving for.

Once, years later, he brought up the fact that others had asked him about marrying again. He said, "After you've been shipwrecked and washed ashore, you don't go looking for another boat." By that, he meant his will was gone; after loving someone like that and experiencing tremendous loss, something sacred is extinguished, and the place where the love lived gets tired and grows cold. I have often wondered if all of us have just been wandering through the world since Mama died—unable to fully risk knowing love again at all.

Beatrice, our housekeeper, was there to help Mama, and to take care of you, too, Benbrook House. Though the older children seemed to love her, I was too young to not be intimidated by her somewhat scowling face. She meant no harm; she'd just had a hard life and didn't feel like smiling much.

In the only picture I have of her, I can see the visible dissatisfaction on her face that seemed to settle like a cloud over all of us. Few were allowed inside your walls at Benbrook, but Beatrice was one of them in the earlier years. Though I did not feel connected to her, she was one of us.

By the time I was an adult, I realized what you had meant to me. My most cherished and haunted memories were bound together by your rooms, in a mental scrapbook. You saw the best and worst of Mama—watched her nestle in beside me, beneath thick quilts, when her love was tangible and easy for me to touch, and after she'd withered away, when your insulation became paper thin, and all the days felt like a desolate winter.

During her peak, we'd gather around the piano to listen to her play—something ethereal that would awaken the most sentimental parts of our spirit. And we would worship her, as the sound of our small voices would ricochet off your walls, creating a memory so valuable and haunting, we would never escape it.

Phoebe in front of Mama's piano, 1970

For Mother in the Last and Early Years

At Benbrook,
The walls were rotting.
But the children sang.

Pots were banged and there was brightness in places.
The piano swelled and pushed us against our walls of paper.
But for every piano key touched,
Its player
Began a complete and slow unwinding.

Key by key, note by note, bar by bar;
For every triumphant chord struck,
The eyes widened and then stared,
Till they no longer heard the music.
But there was the music.

And the feet pumped madly at the pedals.
And the hands swept up and down again.
And there were sweats and snuffs and grunts,
And hoots with music—
Hoo hoo *said the hair,*
And it was the last place the madness swept,
Through kinky black and grey,
And lifted each strand high.

We resisted no more, but rose and

Embraced it.

Bare feet gliding over the wooden floor in and out,

And in and out of one another's arms.

Till we fell and ended in a crescendo of feet beat—

Converts, all of us,

Pounding and hollering to the religion of Katherine.

CHAPTER 5

Dear Man on the Street Bench

Dear Man on the Street Bench,

It was a dark night, fifty years ago, and you'd been drinking. I wonder if you remember me. It's possible, but perhaps not probable. You must have been thirty years my senior the night we met, as far as my four-year-old eyes could discern.

We never learned each other's names. But I've carried you with me all this time, just as my mother carried me to the street bench that night—and left me. I've even written a poem about you, wondered if I cast you appropriately, marveled at the reality that you might have been dangerous, or just as reasonably an angel sent to save me, and acknowledged I will never know.

On the night in question, I woke up in the arms of my mother as she walked in the dark of night on our street. She carried me across her body in her arms, as she navigated the sidewalk up Benbrook Boulevard toward the Bluebonnet Circle. After a few moments, I was awake enough to walk on my own, so she put me on the ground, and we traveled the remaining quarter mile hand in hand.

Before we arrived to the bus stop at Bluebonnet Circle, we stopped at the Dairy Queen next door for a vanilla ice milk with a cone that tasted more like paper. There, Mama was busy organizing—coordinating. I knew this from her energy, although she spoke no words to this effect. This was not our first night trip to Bluebonnet Circle; there had been others.

On one earlier trip, she told me to pack all of my favorite things: my Minnie Mouse doll, my patent leather dress-up boots, and my black purse that was covered in embroidered flowers and opened with a fancy gold hinge. I did, only for her to ask me to abandon them in the gas station bathroom abruptly when *plans changed*, promising me we would go back for them. We never went back.

Even at four, this did not make sense to me. *Why would we not have ample room to carry only a few items with us? Where were we going?*

That night Mama called friends. They came in their car. We left. Without the toys. I grieved losing them and wondered, over the years, where they'd ended up.

But on this night's outing, we made no stop at the gas station, as it was torn down now and a Dairy Queen was built in its place. We went inside the Dairy Queen and ordered a cone of soft serve ice cream—a rare treat. Then, we headed out to the street bench by the bus stop, somewhere between twilight and midnight. Without much explanation, Mama left me there, promising to *be back soon.*

As usual, I said very little. I knew better than to argue or add drama to the situation. With ten kids, no one needed to be ushering in chaos and complication. Especially not *Baby Phoebe*—favored for being the littlest. Ten children having their own needs is a struggle all its own. Curtailing my feelings as always, I braced my bottom against the back of the street bench and ate my ice cream.

Then you came. I willed you to say something to me, to ask me why I was there, to question why I was alone. Even at that age, I knew it was not normal that I would be on a bench by myself at night, so it seemed odd when you came that we sat in silence. You were a grown-up, and I was a little girl. I assumed that meant that you would do something very adult, like ask me how I was doing, ask if I was okay. Your energy was slow and nonthreatening. I was not afraid, just disappointed that you had chosen not to talk.

I looked at you out of the corner of my eye; you looked back, but your eyes were far away. You stayed silent and took a pull from your bottle. We sat there in the quiet long enough for me to finish my ice cream but not eat the empty cone.

Horns honked. Headlights flashed in our eyes. She was not coming. We still said nothing.

Then Mama was back. She scooped me up and we headed back inside the store, where she asked the man to refill my cone for being *a good girl.* I was glad everything was okay again, whatever that meant for our dynamic.

In any case, Mr. Man on the Street Bench, I like to believe that you were sent to protect me. Though you said nothing, your silence communicated everything. I intuited that you understood what it felt like to be lonely maybe, going through something difficult—like the rest of us. It was far better to have had you there than to not have had you. Even better, you sat yourself not too far away beside me, and you didn't leave.

Thank you for never leaving me, even after all these years.

The Street Bench

On the bench, I thought about the bloody opossums.

When she left me there, she said,
"Stay here. I'll be back."
And I stood and locked my legs,
So that my bottom was braced against the bench back.

The cone, because I was good, was there with me.
After she left, I plunged my mouth on the crest of the cone,
Making the ice cream bigger and bigger,
Till it was bigger than the night and my aloneness.

A black man with a bottle came to sit on the bench.
I opened my eyes but he said nothing.
I looked off to where she had gone, to make him
more comfortable.
That didn't make him say anything.

Lick. Not anything.
Lick. A horn honked.
Lick. Not her.
I looked hard at the man to make him say something.

He still didn't say anything.
He drank from his bottle.

Lick. She
Lick. Was
Lick. Not coming.
The man did not care except for his bottle.
Lick. Lick. Lick.
Lick. Or. Liquor.
I swallowed ice cream on top of the cry bubble and it
went down.
At the bottom of my cone was a bloody opossum.

When she came back, she hugged me and swept me up.
We went back inside the store so the man
Could swirl more soft cream inside my cone.
I ate through the cream again,
And was disappointed to find at the bottom—
A bloody opossum.

CHAPTER 6

Dear Dad

Dear Dad,

I am fifty-four years old now, and I am writing this to thank you for being both a mother and a father to the ten of us. You never considered walking out the door, not on your own children and not on the others who were not your blood but who believed in you. Though other fathers of the '70s often chose to abandon their homes, you stayed. You were impervious to anyone who judged you, although you were, for the most part, highly regarded within our school community for being a single father who was raising his kids.

Maybe there were some distant, wealthy churchgoing moms who judged you for not attending Sunday services, for not *knowing God.* Instead, you hung light and still like a prism, as God moved through you—casting miracles and hope where we needed it. Your love was the kind we could count on.

You kept to yourself in your shop in the backyard on Benbrook Boulevard, with tools displayed and hung all around on pegboards or other wooden mounts that you had designed and constructed. Your workbench had a million pockmarks, and a clamp mounted on the end that you must have used a thousand times when making furniture and other projects. There was often sawdust on the floor, and always an inspiring piece in the works, like the beautiful writing desk with cabinets that you made for us one Christmas.

If not wood, you were working with clay to sculpt a portrait bust of one of us Popes, or with oils on canvas. Other times it was jewelry, and occasionally iron work with your forge. The shop is where you went to find both relief from your grief and melancholic inspiration. You were disciplined about work projects and would rise very early to begin.

When you were sad, you wrote beautiful poems about the Trinity River and intriguing murder mysteries, holding everything loosely and releasing it back into the atmosphere, the way you continually released Mama.

I think that's why she migrated to you in the dimly lit club in Taos. It was your creativity and the innate promise you carried of something more that drew her into conversation with you, near the stage, as you both examined the lonely guitar player's Martin strings. Her heart was captivated by how you were free *and* safe—never caring about superficial things, only caring about the things that mattered.

I am sorry you lost the love of your life, over and over again; that your dreams didn't turn out as you'd hoped; that your marriage, which, in another era, might have been sustainable, devolved into something utterly tragic. You lost your partner—mentally, virtually, and physically. You had work friends but no friends to truly lean on, because that was not in your nature. And family was not an option with your father and mother living in Florida, and for the most part estranged. You'd spent your whole life losing—your sister, who had passed away, and your brother, who was merely a shadow in the family.

You were an innate hard worker—at both masculine and feminine tasks. Neither you nor Mama was ever confined by the gender roles of the time, back when women were knocked out with anesthesia to give birth and husbands were not allowed in the birthing room. You ushered us into adulthood and sowed into our wellbeing and character what it meant *to be okay*.

It was evident you couldn't save Mama, although you tried. Though we Three Popes were too little to talk about it at the time, you admitted to me later that you thought it was her hysterectomy that made her go crazy. You suffered alone and were unable to process with anyone. We longed to offer you comfort—even your stepchildren, save Patricia, found great solace in you.

I understand Patricia's pain, that she needed to put the blame on someone else. She'd taken Mama away, thinking she could save her, needing to be able to do something constructive in a situation that was becoming increasingly tragic. She needed someone to blame for Mama being alive one moment, and then being gone, all on her watch. It was no one's fault, but she tried to place the brunt of it on you, though I think we've all learned by now that you can't save someone no matter how much you love them—no matter how diligently you try, *no matter*. You tried.

After Mama was gone, your routine was long and laborious. You often made hot cereals for breakfast, and on Monday mornings would rise at five to head to the Washateria to do laundry. You always dropped us off at school in the baby blue Rambler station wagon, and we began walking home together at an early age. Once we arrived back home to 2701 Benbrook Boulevard, we'd play as we pleased, both inside and out. You taught us how to use our imagination and that it was the one thing that could rescue us from the troubles of the world.

On the weekends, you'd take us to flea markets, where we would buy sugarcane and sometimes arrowheads. On other occasions, you'd take us to the museums and we'd wander for hours behind you, studying each painting. Usually, we would get to choose a postcard of our favorite painting from the gift shop before we left.

When the weather was warm, we'd slice the day open like an orange and take the dogs to the park beneath the wide-open Texas sky. We'd bring bread and cheese that would melt in the sun, and sodas that weren't cold but were good anyway. Our special trips involved long drives out into the country to see the Big Black Bull.

In certain years, when we were little, we took turns sleeping with you. Because *I was the littlest,* I usually got to sleep with you more often than the others. I would fall asleep much easier on those nights.

Very early on, you began to tell us about Sam, the character from the movie you wrote, *Don't Look in the Basement,* which, when it was released in 1973, grossed $40 million at the drive-ins.

You weren't especially proud of it, nor were you pleased that you were only paid $800 to write the script, but you were approached by the director, and so you said yes.

The best part of the project, though, was that Bill McGhee, the actor who played Sam, became a friend to us in real life. We were comforted by the way he was made alive by you, and that he was also an underdog and an unlikely hero. It was unbelievable that there could be a hero at all in the story of a corrupt mental ward where patients posed as doctors to act out murder and mayhem. In the end, Sam was the only one with a true moral code—which pointed him back to sanity.

Sam was a healing presence to us in the house at Benbrook Boulevard. He must have been a healing presence to you as well. You'd written the script on the heels of Mama's death—it was no coincidence that you created a story about mental illness with at least one redemptive arc.

Years later, we realized that the movie was a hit, in part, because mental illness was beginning to be a circulating subject within the social consciousness. It was obviously one in our house as well at the time that you wrote the script. When you finally met Bill at your joint birthday party with my daughter, Sarah Katherine, in 2007, you were moved by how far your creativity had come to life. The gesture seemed appropriate after I'd met him at a local screening of your film. I invited him and his daughter over to meet the man who'd dreamed up one of the most important characters of his acting career. What a great day that was.

When we were little, you never criticized us or mandated expectations. You were always supportive with your words and energy—you believed in us. We understood our worth because of you; you never left us to wonder if we were loved.

Our seventh-grade teacher once remarked on how well we all spoke the "King's English." No, we'd never been taught how to eat properly from a soup bowl as you had been forced to do, but you taught us how to speak well and articulate our truth. You had a way of only giving us what was made to last. You were gentle and understood the delicate nature of a child's psyche, spirit, and intelligence.

We were taught to cultivate our gifts, to *play* in our work. I realize now that the jobs you held at the Museum of Science and History and the Fort Worth Zoo were for us. They were the perfect places for children of a single parent to grow up and explore.

We couldn't afford much, but you made sure there was money for museum school, which included pottery and rock-polishing classes and trips to see the dinosaur tracks in Glen Rose. We also got to do a lot of exploring of the exhibits behind the scenes at the museum where you worked. We got to see the tarantulas, and even the little red fox, up close.

Later during the zoo years, we Three Popes were invited to be volunteer workers; we even got special name tags. We were trained to clean *The Three Little Pigs* exhibit in the children's zoo; fed the sea lions; played with Benny the Baby Elephant; and even got to keep a tiny guinea pig in our coat pocket for the full day, as long as we returned it to its proper place before quitting time. We had so many privileges—because of *you*.

During the summer after sixth grade, we took a trip to San Antonio that we were barely able to afford. The train dropped us off, literally on the tracks, and we had to carry our suitcases a long way before we could hail a taxi. That night, after spending the day at the Alamo, you took us to the revolving restaurant. I'd put my purse on the ledge and was fearful that I'd lost it. Forty-five minutes later, it circled its way back around to the other side of the building and I gratefully grabbed it. Being able to make that trip was a really big deal. It meant a lot to me, Dad.

Your parents occasionally financed a trip to Naples, Florida, for us. Those trips were hardly a vacation for you, but you endured them for our sake. We Three Popes got a lot of your mom's sweet energy. We were kept by her in a neat and tidy house. We had our very own twin beds to sleep in and homemade ham salad to eat. In the afternoon, we'd play cards with your mother's sister-in-law, our Aunt Marion, from next door. She was as gentle as the day is long, and we trusted and loved her.

While we were having fun swimming in the ocean, you were doing due diligence with your father—listening, conversing, striving, but never being heard or approved of. You had no one to give you strength, so you were your own strength—and our strength as well. You grieved the early death of your sister Abby during those trips—still amazed that she'd never uttered a word before three years of age, due to family dysfunction that yielded a delay in her development. You also lamented Billy and the scandal he'd brought to the family, with his string of broken relationships and estranged children. I'd never met him, but you spoke of him as though he was different than you: handsome, charismatic, devilish, and seeking opportunity everywhere he could. Your motive was always about creating opportunity—for us.

In eighth grade, we three Pope siblings got a scholarship to Mexico. We thought we'd won the lottery; in a sense, we had. Because we were good students, Ms. Rayel applied on our behalf, and we each paid only $50 for a whole month of studying in Cuernavaca while being hosted by a family. And that included plane fare!

While we were gone, you redid the house at Benbrook—painted our bedrooms, hung curtains, and made everything *new*. You primed us with a fresh coat of paint, a bright beginning, and something to look forward to as we entered high school. It gave us the feeling of being like everyone else, and indeed, ninth grade was the first time we invited friends into the house again after Mama's death.

You brought many unique people into our lives because they were drawn to you, including Mike Bell: zookeeper and unlikely family friend. In our college years, you relayed the news of his tragic death to Mary and me, while we were on an immersion trip to Mexico. His death was brutal and made the headlines. He was knocked down by an Asian bull elephant and crushed. We grieved. The Fort Worth Zoo put up a statue in his memory.

It meant everything that you befriended him, Dad. Especially because Mike Bell was a hard person to move toward. He had a foul mouth and braggartly ways, but you saw through all of that. You knew he really just needed companionship, and so we brought your turkey and stuffing to him at the zoo on Thanksgiving because he didn't have the day off—or any family with whom to celebrate the holiday. We watched him eat the huge turkey leg and then demolish the bones. I'm pretty sure he just wanted to shock us.

Over the years, we Three Popes broke through his bluster and eventually warmed to him, and in my last years of high school, I ran into him at one of the zookeeper parties. He gave me his business card that read *Dr. Zoo* and told me I could call him if I ever needed help. I believed him, no doubt, in that moment, and could sense how much it meant to him that we were family friends. We were all the same kind of outsiders, and somehow it made for something stronger than a usual friendship.

Times got easier for you when we were in high school—maybe. With two teens of my own, I wonder if it was hard on you to watch us grow up as time passed after Mama's death. Grief is interesting that way: first you grieve the event, then you grieve the anniversary of the event, then you grieve the time that has passed since the event, and then you grieve how you feel like you're never *all there* when you should be—out of body, like the world went on without you, without your loved one, so cruelly that you just stopped.

In our high school years, there were so many vulnerable young people in our house and so many opportunities to venture into late night parties and poor decisions—all possible paths to a permanently wrong future. You'd already lost so much. I'm sure there was a temptation to worry. But instead, you followed your pattern of trusting, and we responded by keeping our grades up and maintaining jobs.

Our teen friends loved our house because of its realness, something lacking at times in their own homes, and would flock to hang out with us in our upstairs. You went to bed early every night, leaving us to be the teens we were and drink beer as teens do. I remember you getting up only once when things got too loud. Your roar sent everyone fleeing in fear—down the stairs and out the front door and into the neighbors' yard. On more than one occasion, though, I chose to yank beer cans out of disrespectful visitors' hands when they'd help themselves to your Texas Pride. Money was scant, and I was protective of you affording your fixed number of beers every night. No one faulted you for that, and you never, ever lost control.

After we graduated high school, Mary and I attended Austin College. You moved to Mississippi, and William joined you. Together, you built the beautiful house you had dreamed of in Guntown, not far away from the Mississippi coast of Biloxi. You'd fallen in love with it when you were stationed there as a young man, an early husband, and a new father. It was the last place you'd had the indulgence of unfettered joy and vision, so you made it beautiful, with intricate beaded woodwork, perfectly pasted wallpaper, a studio with a glass wall, and a kitchen, complete with a fireplace. It was a charming house, every detail. You loved baking bread in the kitchen while stoking flames in the hearth to warm the room, eating soup with a proper spoon in a proper manner, if you chose.

Kevin and I came to visit after we were married, to bless it with the help of our hands and make it even more of a home. We set up cot beds to sleep out on the screened-in porch, and by morning, we were surrounded by large, fuzzy cows—peacefully forming a wall of warmth and breath while we dreamed. They were only feet away—hard to say how long they were there, but for certain they enjoyed being with us. They chose it.

I never said so, but I felt Abigail's energy there with us that morning when we awoke. I had mourned Mama's loss of our baby sister, and as an adult, I grieved it in a new way. Abigail's spirit was strong, peaceful, and serene that morning with the cows in Mississippi. She was there for you, Dad. She came for you. I felt it.

It's hard to think of the house that you and William lovingly built with your two hands belonging to a new family now, on the twenty beautiful acres in rural Mississippi. Through it, you'd also worked on rebuilding your relationship with him, healing from the fact that you'd both been treated like second-class citizens by the strong-willed women in the family.

Isn't it true that as you dug the foundation and picked up the hammers to swing, you felt a little more compassion for yourselves, and for each other? That your hearts opened, once again, just a little bit and that you hoped again for closeness? You spoke without words, helped each other through silence with rhythm and intention—and the bond followed.

I believe Abigail watches over what you left behind; the title may no longer be in our name, but that property and house will forever belong to what you built in the spirit of our family. In the same way that we belong to you. Every Pope. Every Harris. Every Mason.

We are forever your pillars and beams, because you were our first firm foundation. I think Sam is on the property in Mississippi, too, Dad. It makes sense that he would stay, for you, who gave up your whole life for your creativity, and for us.

And so, I write this for you, whose love still endures, long after life left your lungs and you transcended this place to go home, and to go *back to Mama*.

Missing You

I miss you.

It is strange to welcome this pain that comes,
Welcome it, because it is the only means to know you again.
My humanness makes it impossible sometimes to
Remember your smell;

To access the core of me,
Tied to the core of you,
Bonded through cold winters, our poorness, empty pantries
that even the roaches no longer visited,

Remembering the feel of icy air in your shop
Amidst dogs and dust and 7-Eleven coffee;

Watching you select a prized tool,
Then head, again, to the pawnshop.

You gave me life, but never with it was the
Cheap promise of easy.

I stood by you, knowing the pact of our hard life,
Committed to waking with worry;
To knowing that most of the day would be filled with
insecurities for both of us.

I did not question the terms, knowing only that your promise
Was good and forever.

And I knew, deep down, that even if a door had been open
You never would have left.

That is why, now, I feel it absolutely critical
To remember the smell of your shirt.

I feel my life depends upon remembering the smell of
your shirt.

Tim Pope and first wife, Leandra McCormack, Wedding Day, 1952

Trip to Naples, Florida, to see our Pope grandparents, 1970s

Dad's father, mother, and Placebo the dog

With Dad's father, Robert Pope, in Florida

The twins in matching yellow shirts

CHAPTER 7

Dear Patricia

Dear Patty,

You were my eldest sister, twenty-one years my senior. The one whom I did not know well, who would show up every now and again, at our dining table, with fellow intellectual and husband, David Gilmartin.

I familiarized myself with you only through your letters. You loved to write, as Mama did, and your handwriting was similar to hers—it was the part of her you kept with you, and gave to us, after she left this world in your home. At her funeral, many states away, you were angry at Dad and angry at the world. Dad decided that we young children should not attend the service; he believed we would not be able to make sense of it.

Every time you made an appearance in our lives, you were more human than the image I had of you—shopping for new jeans and a matching plaid shirt to fold into a pretty package that you would send for my birthday in the mail. Your gifts always came when clothing was scarce. I knew you cared for me, sympathized that we had little, and attempted to soothe the loss through letters.

Before Mama died, you and David would pop by the Benbrook house with your children: Alice, Jenny, and Aaron. They were roughly the age of us Three Popes. Then, after Mama's death, when you visited Texas you'd stay at Mama Harris's house on Rogers Street near the University church. When we would arrive for a visit, Aaron, your baby—younger than me by only a few months—would call out,

"Mom! The kids are here!"

Which would irritate William to no end, since as the uncle, he was older than Aaron, if only by a year and a half.

I felt that I got to know you more as I became an adult, largely through phone calls and the occasional package in the mail, which all felt personal, like a warm hug.

You were one of the Mason children, the first of my siblings, and daughter of Jesse Mason, whom we once traveled to Denton together to visit. He seemed pleasant enough, *simple* as Mama had always described him, while still *absent*, as you had experienced him during your upbringing. I can't imagine what it felt like to have lost Mama at twenty-six after having a father who chose to not be there for you as well; it makes sense that you would resent Dad. He was the only grown-up still around to hate.

As an adult, you took your husband's last name. After your divorce, you opted to be Patricia Mason—your Dad's daughter—once more. Johnny, your biological brother, chose to take the name of your stepfather—Joe Harris—at least for a few years anyway. But you didn't. You decided it was better to take a man's name who was never there for you than to take the name of the man who is rumored to have stolen your innocence.

It scares me to imagine what you and our Harris sisters went through at the hands of Joe Harris, another family secret we all keep—memories that are ours, but are not ours. You couldn't save yourself, and you valued strong coping skills after it was all over. I remember the many conversations in which you would express, in loving and subtle ways, that you wished your children might develop some of the survival instincts that William, Mary, and I had adopted over the years.

I know you, being an older sibling, were sometimes surprised by the way the three youngest siblings grew up—forced to grow strong in response to the adversities. We were not really aware of it. Mama carried you in her first marriage; you'd grown up in an entirely different household, a different socioeconomic class. Maybe you had nice dresses, summers full of sweet tea, dance classes, sunshine; maybe they were easier days. I can only surmise.

Fun, I suppose, was packaged for you by the simplicity of childhood. I hope there were carefree days for you before Mama and your father, Jesse, split up. We Popes had mostly only known hardship. Dad taught us how to make our fun with books, drawing, whittling wood with our pocketknives, using our imaginations to stay engaged and occupied. And perhaps, some of our imagining served just to escape the hardship—maybe that was part of the survival that kept us seamlessly together through years of having very little.

You always called on the holidays—Thanksgiving specifically. You tried to stay current, even in between. As adults, we talked about parenthood, until finally I gave you a pill that was too hard to swallow. I told you that I believed your kids should be helping you, instead of you helping them so much. Sadly, it was too much truth for our relationship; we could no longer keep our heads afloat. Regrettably, we talked very little after that.

Within months of our final conversation, we got the call from David Gilmartin that you had passed unexpectedly at the age of sixty-seven in your car, after getting some Asian soup for dinner. You were headed home. After getting into the car, and buckling yourself in, your heart simply gave out.

Yours and David's commitment to your children was inspiring; they were highly creative like Mama and cultivated their gifts. They grew to be gifted musicians, gifted speakers, and highly dimensional in their thinking. They thrived in their creative endeavors but sometimes struggled at life skills.

Your and David's investment in the Waldorf School helped your children have the same hands-on, Montessori learning experience that Mama offered to her students and her own children. It was an education that encouraged permanent learning through the five senses, inner discipline, and maximum development of creativity through artistic expression in everyday life.

I admire the work you achieved in your later years, in the areas of mental health, while in pursuit of your PhD. When you passed, you were working at Boeing, offering vocational counseling to employees. It less than thrilled you, because by that time you had realized that no amount of studies or caring offered you the opportunity to save another person. We can only save ourselves in the end—if that—and that is a fortunate ending.

I wondered when you left Earth if things had gotten to be too much for you. I kept thinking: *If only I'd fully understood you. If only we could have been closer. If only I'd listened better.*

Perhaps, when you spoke of your children, what you couldn't say is that you were worried that one might actually be as vulnerable as Mama, and the idea that you couldn't save her was too terrible to face.

Like all of us, you hold some of Mama's best traits—her bright, beautiful intelligence. Kate and Steph, who knew you most, miss you terribly. You were a wonderful older sister to them. You were strong. I understand if you felt very guilty about Mama's death and if the only way to resolve that was to pointedly blame Dad for taking her life. It was no one's fault.

Yet, to have to verbalize and to accept that she died on your watch, after you had taken her into your home to protect her, might have given you too many *if onlys* to hold. It was too much.

Ironically, I'd never learned the true story of Mama's death until after my son, Elijah, was born. When we attended William's wedding to Adria in Taos, your ex-husband, David Gilmartin, finally shared the story personally with Mary—told her that he had driven Mama to the hospital and dropped her off at the emergency room, after she'd already swallowed the pills.

She had already tried to overdose several times; I imagine David was tired of the burden of taking care of someone in such a fractured mental state. I don't blame him for that.

In any case, I learned at thirty-three years old that Mama did not die quietly in her sleep the way Dad had told me when I was five. Instead, she died alone in the emergency room, screaming in pain, unable to reverse the actions she was desperate to undo, as she begged God to live.

I'm sorry, Patricia. I can't imagine how vacant your home felt after she was gone, and what it must have been like to tell the family about her death. You must have been tormented. I cannot help but wonder if that was a large part of the reason why you and David divorced. What marriage could hold that? To be a constant reminder for the other brings far too much pain. You both did the best you could, Patricia. We all did.

Believing you did your best requires me to give you the benefit of the doubt for reaching out to Betty Carter when we Three Popes were third graders, living with her temporarily. I'm not sure how you happened to contact her but clearly you gave her an earful about Dad to turn her from being an ally to an enemy. She went from being a friendly Cub Scout co-parent, offering to help the single dad neighbor who had just lost his job, to a full-on adversary. What did you tell her, Patricia? Did you say he was a horrible drunk who was responsible for my mother's death, and that we should be taken from him?

Meanwhile, you couldn't have known that Mr. Carter, her husband, was putting his hands where they didn't belong on both Mary and me. That late at night, when he came to tuck us in, he wore a tank top and nothing else, then leaned over us as he said good night, as his nakedness dangled right in our faces. You couldn't have known that Betty Carter was giving her son John French kissing lessons as we Three Popes watched. We were young at the time, but knew better than to consider her behavior *normal*, even if she was laughing. Even if she said it was *only a joke*. You couldn't have known about the things that just *should not have been.*

When William ran away because he hated living with Betty Carter,

Betty tried to tell you it was because he was a *bad little boy*. The truth is that Betty would dart around the house, with covetous purpose, a licensed busybody, whispering urgently into the phone under her breath—so Mary and I couldn't hear—vilifying Dad until it was so unbearable that William chose to run away. He fled because he knew the energy at the Carters' was wrong; he fled because the words you shared with Betty Carter bound us there, because your good intentions shadowed the truth for us, and we were forbidden to go home. Benbrook Boulevard was only one block over. Betty Carter, out of the blue, said there would be no more crossing the street, cutting through the neighbor's yard, sneaking down the alley, then scaling the fence to see Dad.

Betty Carter gave us no explanation for her rules, and no room to speak on Dad's behalf. So the Father's Day card that I made him—telling him how much I missed him—that I planned to give him in person, went undelivered. I remember thinking that he would never understand why I chose not to show up on Father's Day; it broke my heart that we couldn't be there for him—we had always made Father's Day a very special celebration.

There was no way to tell him what was happening. We didn't have a phone, and we certainly weren't confiding anything in Betty. It was a very traumatic few weeks of my young life. We Three Popes had managed to survive in our pain without Mama, but living without Dad was out of the question.

Betty Carter insisted that we were *better off* without the man who gave everything he had to make things right, working for minimal pay, to help us make ends meet; *better off* without the man who'd tried his best to make a home for suffering children; *better off* without the father who'd always put the needs of those he loved over his own. *Better off*—with her.

You could not have known that I ran away despite the rules, sobbing and running as fast as I could to reach Dad, falling face forward over the fence but continuing anyway, blinded by my own tears, on a steady mission to get to him. To Dad, whom Betty Carter covertly threatened with her malicious lies in her false effort to protect us. To Dad, the only person who would never hurt us. To Dad, the only person on whom we could depend.

Arriving home and finding the house empty was more than I could bear. *Dad.* I knew there was something very, very out of place for him to not be there. I'll never know this for sure, but looking back now, I think Dad may have been off on a legal errand at that exact moment, fighting for justice, ensuring Betty Carter could do no more harm to our family. That same day, when I had to return to the Carters', I chose in the blink of that specific moment to lean into God. I walked back to the Carters' from our house with a quiet prayer that we would soon be returned—and allowed myself to fully trust. A few weeks later, we were home to Benbrook Boulevard for good.

Patricia, I love you. I forgive you for never asking me, *Phoebe*, about my experience. I forgive you for befriending Betty Carter, who was no friend to us. I wish you'd heard our stories. I wish you'd known our pain. I kept thinking: *if Patty would just ask me, then I could tell her the truth.*

But you couldn't have known that.

If only.

Mama with Patricia and Johnny, Fort Worth, Texas, 1949

Siblings at Will and Adria's wedding

Family photo in Taos

CHAPTER 8

Dear Johnny

Dear Sweet Johnny, who has always had the energy of a faithful child,

Doesn't God say to come to him as a child or you will not enter into the Kingdom of Heaven?

I've never known you to be anything but gentle, so it was hard to believe the stories I'd heard as a teenager, about how you and Dad didn't get along. Perhaps it's because you're a Mason. Maybe you missed your own dad.

Whatever the case—I never minded sharing my dad with you, because you were always kind to me, and vulnerable. We were *the special two*. I was Mama's favorite as *the baby*, and in another world, and another generation, you were her *special boy*. You were almost twenty years my senior.

You and Mama resonated with each other because you were musically gifted, and you both had a heart for theater. When you were hardly a teen, Mama cast you in the leading part in Huck Finn, at Casa Mañana, with Dad playing your father, and your performance was so enchanting they cast you in a commercial for the playhouse. When you grew up, you shared your talents with many, and brought beauty into your corner of the world through your work—including the years when you and Peter, and sometimes Ben and William, entertained crowds with guitars and banjos on Taos Square.

Your circle of friends there knew you. It was a safe place you could openly share your vulnerabilities and celebrate your gifts with other equally creative minds. The famous Taos artist RC Gorman was always a good friend to you. He knew your delicate nature and understood the psyche of an artist. Everyone was gentle with you, Johnny, because you were pure intentioned and always easy on the ears and heart.

You and Liz joined together in this lifetime for as long as you both could manage. From your union, you had Aubri Dai, my goddaughter—who is bright, shining, plucky, and beautiful. She is your legacy. Her goodness came from you.

I didn't know you much in my younger years, Johnny—and wonder if you felt close to me. I was too young to remember you being at home with us, and by the time I was old enough to learn about you, you'd already moved away. It wasn't until I was a teen that I began to know your personality. Somehow it's an odd age to begin a relationship.

I will never forget the night I began my running regime, as a teenager in high school, after considering for so long that I desperately needed an outlet besides beer, something to make me mentally healthy. Running called to me, even though I had no running shoes.

I'd gone out earlier in the evening—probably even had a few beers. But in the way of teenagers, at 2:00 a.m. I decided there was no better time to start my new routine than the present. I ran from our house all the way up Merida and down Berry Street, then all the way to Mama Harris's house, which was only two blocks away from TCU.

I'll never forget arriving, having told no one where I was going. And there you were—waiting for me, in the dead of early morning. You said,

"Phoebe, I've been waiting for you so that we could run."

Something connected us that night. Just that once. It was a moment I'll always remember—so far-fetched and ethereal, yet neither of us questioned it, because in all the ways the moment made no sense, it made perfect sense.

So we ran together, you and me, me in my shoes that were not running shoes. You, who as far as I know, were not a runner—not then, not now. We ran as far as we could go. It was something unexplainable. Natural. Supernatural. Perhaps it was Mama, running right through us, saving us from something, ourselves, the shadow parts of her. Who will ever know what her sacred purpose was that night, in bringing us together?

I've always trusted your energy, Johnny, always known you were a good soul. It's felt good to keep you supplied with your supplement needs over these last years. Ever since you entered the group home in Colorado, I've been sending you ginkgo biloba and probiotics, which you take religiously for your mental health. I like to support you in that effort, in the midst of your mental struggles. You have been constant in your commitment to yourself and disciplined in taking the vitamins that are critical for your brain's wellbeing.

At one point in your life, you told me that you had *chosen* to be mentally ill. I marveled at the selection of your words, but I knew what you said was true, and the honesty and clarity of your thought was powerful.

I've witnessed this in others: when we make a series of small choices to not care for ourselves, it can result in self-sabotage and throw the mind completely out of balance, from which one cannot always recuperate without help.

And so, I help you, Johnny, to take the steps of self-care, so that you can stay in balance, so you can stay on this side of the downward spiral. *So far, so good.*

You've been on medication for years, Johnny, and I've often wondered if they were the cure or the cause. I've feared the latter, while celebrating that pills never took you from me, the way they took Mama. You have remained your sweet and true self, and even though you have struggled privately, in the context of your own mind, you've continued offering your music to the world and being prayerful with those around you.

The moments when we've talked and prayed together have meant a lot, especially your recent phone call to me in which you expressed your anguish over the way you treated Dad. I remember telling you that you could just speak it out to him, that he would be listening, and that he certainly was not holding any grudges. Dad, of all people, would be the first to understand teenage behavior and would also be the first to forgive it.

I remember us praying together when we talked to Dad and asked him to give you the peace and knowingness that he loved you. I stood in the room where he died when we prayed, and I felt his presence. I looked over to the very first painting that I painted when I was with him—in his studio, in Mississippi. It was a monochromatic portrait of Pablo Picasso. I still love its strength, and how it came together with ease, as though it was being painted through me.

It was also the painting that fell from the wall the first and only time I asked Dad to show me his presence in his spirit form. He showed me.

He was there with us that day and we lifted you up, Johnny. I knew because your heart was quieted a bit and a divine peace came over you. That was the divine apex moment *from* Dad—our moment of praying together. Healing.

I love you, Johnny, in this life and in the next. There, you can teach me to play the banjo on the other side of the rainbow bridge.

You have calmed me and enchanted me with your music, the Johnny Harris-produced CD "Voice of the Big Guitar." "Pancho and Lefty," performed by you and Peter, has always been a piece that stirs my heart. If I go before you, please usher me out with that song. If you go before me, you'll hear me singing, "Not his mama's only boy but her favorite one it seems. She began to cry when he said goodbye—sank into his dreams."

God bless you, Johnny the good, Johnny the child, Johnny the dreamer.

The Brothers on Taos Square, 1980

CHAPTER 9

Dear Taos Land

Dear Taos Land,

You are abiding, unfaltering, in all of us, and we belong to you.

I am the youngest daughter of Katherine Jeanne Allred Pope and Timothy Sheldon Pope and of no relation to the other *supposed* co-owner of the land, my mother's second husband, Joseph Robert Harris. I've heard about his wanton evil ways, his propensity for drink. It is tucked away in all ten siblings—wrapped in various layers of our individual bodies in ways that we've all quietly been forced to preserve. I see the wounds in my brothers and sisters that were catalyzed by Joe's sickness. But, if there's one thing I know about land, it's that it can be broken, fed, regenerated, tilled, and *healed.*

In reflecting on our family history, there are three legacies that immediately come to mind. The first is the legacy of the art that our parents lived and brought to life. It has manifested in my siblings, in their children, in their children's children, and in my own kids.

Although not all of us were educated in Montessori schools, we were brought up by our parents, who embodied the life philosophy of Montessori: honoring the blueprint within every child, celebrating the perfect potential that lies inside, and cultivating the environment to invite expressions of creativity in the everyday. Together, my mother and father created Ideas in Motion, a Montessori school that invited this for other children as well.

Our parents were makers, musicians, playwrights, authors, poets, and painters. They have cultivated their gifts, and their dreams have come to fruition from seeds sown in faith.

The second legacy that I would name would be that of the Taos Land that involved the older Mason and Harris children as well as us last-to-be-born Popes. The property was purchased by my mother's parents, *intended for us children*, when she was married to Joe, before she met my father, Timothy Sheldon Pope, on an ethereal night, under the endless New Mexico sky and all its stars.

While my mother's second divorce probably left my older siblings with trembling hands and quaking hearts, I believe it was her third husband—my father—who was sent to redeem the soil in Taos through the trust that he earned from his children.

In listening to the stories of my older brothers and sisters, many come from the time that my family spent together on the Taos property, both before and after I was born. After my mother fled Joe Harris and married my father, I, too, made many trips there, although I was young, and the memories escape me now.

The soil of Taos is embedded in our family history. It involves many summers spent beneath the blistering desert sun that stained our cheeks as we dug our toes into the red dirt to the sound of hammers pounding nails and boards as a house was being built. It saw the death of my father's oldest daughter with my mother. Her name was Abigail, and she died in utero due to a blow to the stomach caused by Mama's former husband, Joe.

Abigail remains buried on the Taos family land today.

Being the youngest of the family, and born to my mother's third husband, I was fortunate in that as a youngster my exposure to Joseph Harris was limited. What was not limited was what I will refer to as the third legacy—the effect of Joe's abusive actions toward his children, my older brothers and sisters.

No doubt, each sister and brother had a unique grief about their painful and damaging memories with Joe. And I have watched all of them emerge into adulthood—and some pass away—still processing the trauma of what happened in their early years for the rest of their lives.

I wonder what it felt like for you to watch us all, toiling, unfolding, raising up a house, rebuilding hearts, generation after generation, father after father.

Man goes back to dust; perhaps it was you who owned us—who was the substance of our skin—as we laughed, played, and cried there. As our parents sweat, worried, and cursed and we children bickered constantly over small hurts that inevitably accumulated into something more. As we struggled to learn, grow, put the pieces back together, and forgive—through many tragedies, but specifically that of sweet, innocent Abigail, the proverbial sacrificial lamb who suffered for others' sins and returned to the ground first. She hovers over the place now, with a still peace about what was.

You knew us better than we knew ourselves, silently and endlessly studying our attributes, character flaws, and iniquities. You knew us each intimately, individually, knew the woman who had a dream of love, who only reaped heartbreak, and then sowed a lifetime of pain for others; you witnessed the men who were fathers, who sometimes did godly deeds, and other times were less than men; you knew my father, who weaved hope into every dead circumstance; you watched Joe Harris, who caused unspeakable pain to the children who loved him.

You were always there, seeing the story begin and end and unfold exactly as it was supposed to. And we broke in your body, built dreams upon it, watched them crumble and regenerate, partook in communion on the land, and spent time there.

A land, a home, belongs to those who spend time there.

Mama and Jody at Taos Land, 1957

Family Bus at Taos Land, Circa 1963

CHAPTER 10

Dear Abigail

Dear Abigail,

Little Sweetness, older than me, but much, much younger than me—

I'm sorry.

Your tiny psyche had not experienced the world, yet you experienced the worst of the world, its very darkest parts. A grown man, in his rage, kicked you, in the sacred space of my mother's womb, hard enough to separate you from her at seven months old. You hemorrhaged and died. Bled to death.

You'd not yet been born, but were fully able to experience pain—more so, in fact, than an older fetus, one who develops neural mechanisms to inhibit pain at thirty-four to thirty-six weeks in utero. So you, little one, suffered more physically, felt more pain, than a full-grown adult would have.

Abigail was a special name because it was the name of Dad's sister, who peculiarly did not speak until she was three, who died an early death as an adult, before you were born. No doubt, Dad wanted to give you the name to heal her spirit, to redeem her death, which came too soon.

It was especially sad then, to add her tragedy to yours.

But of one thing you may take heart, little one—and this you know better than I—as you were returned to the spiritual realm: when a person dies early on this earth, he or she is forever immortalized. You were a beautiful creature, full of purity and innocence that was too young to be tainted. Your gift to those left behind, then, is this legacy of beauty, innocence, and hope. We need this to cling to, to remember, to measure against the darkness—when darkness comes.

JFK, who appointed our Allred grandfather head of the regional SEC, died young; his legacy was much stronger than if he'd lived out the rest of his life, because he is remembered for his youthful optimism, intelligence, and zeal. His physical form is preserved forever as a forty-six-year-old man—an emblem that will endure far more than if he had lived to be one hundred years old. It is the potential that speaks to us, the idea of what could be. In this way, we are kind to those who depart early, with stories unfinished, because it seems we give them the benefit of the doubt, always assuming the best endings to their stories, that they would have remained wholesome and good.

Those who die young fulfill a spiritual purpose; they are the hope bearers for the rest of us; they remind us *how* and *why* to keep living. This hope would not burn through us if it weren't for their fleeting magic. No one can compete with a legend; they keep us moving forward in faith.

Little Abigail, you remain innocent and pure and beautiful, forever and ever, buried under the vast skies of our Taos Land. We will never forget you, and will always wonder about the brilliant life you might have lived. We are grateful you taught us all how to keep moving—especially after Mama died.

When my son, Elijah, was little, he was enamored with the cartoon *Robin Hood.* One day, his concentration broke away from the screen. He looked up at me and asked,

"Mama, what is hot grafonda?" I looked at him, puzzled, wondering if maybe it was a breakfast cereal.

"Where did you hear of it?" I asked him, assuming he was repeating a commercial he'd seen.

"Well, on *Robin Hood,* he always says, *Absence makes the hot grafonda."* I smiled when he said this, and thought of you. Your absence kept us missing the sister we'd never met in person; we felt your spirit despite you never making it to us. I sometimes feel it now.

I know also, little Abigail, that you are with other loved ones—Dad, Mama, Jody, Ben, and Patty. One day, I will meet you, my sister—I cannot wait.

• • •

My departed beloveds have shown me, over and over again, their new realities. When Dad passed, a hummingbird appeared for the first time in our yard, and we knew that it was him, knew that every now and then, God opens a special window for us to feel and experience the spiritual realm, in our deepest grief, and then closes it again.

My cousin, who had lost her father four months earlier, visited me on the day Dad passed. I told her about the hummingbird, and she told me about her father appearing to her as a blackbird, *speaking* excitedly to her on the porch.

Her father, Dick, was Joe Harris's brother. But he was a good man: talented, creative, kind, decent. He knew our father. Later that night, when the morgue came to retrieve Dad's body from our home on Fernald where he passed, I felt a tremendous sense of sadness that his body was being carried out alone, while we were together in a warm house. I comforted myself with the knowingness that his body was not really *him*, that he was with you.

The next morning, I was up early, writing my thoughts for Dad's memorial celebration, when young Elijah came down the stairs.

"Mama!" he said. "Sarah Katherine just saw a hummingbird fly by the window! And he was with a blackbird!"

Neither of my children had heard the story told to me by my cousin. But I understood the significance. My father was letting me know he was not alone. He was with his friend and fellow artist, Dick.

Ben appeared to me often after his passing. I found an inordinate number of articles from him on my early morning runs. I knew instinctively that they all came from him: a perfect copper cross, a beautiful porcelain guitar, a tiny tree of life that appeared on the porch, a pair of golden praying hands in the parking lot. I told my sister that I felt Ben had a vision for us—those were the words I used. Not long after, on a stroll through the neighborhood, I spotted a small rainbow forming—a sign from Ben, I was certain. I then, coincidentally, found a pen lying on the ground with a website name printed on it. When I googled the site, the first thing that popped up was the hymn "Be Thou My Vision."

While this may sound crazy to some, this is usually how the supernatural deals with me—this is how our *beloveds* speak to us.

There are many more stories that make me surer of the divine than even what I experience, on Earth, through my five senses. The other side is real and enduring. And you are part of that knowingness for me, little Abigail, my big sister, whom I never met but will forever feel connected to and will one day meet.

Cow painting in tribute to Abigail

CHAPTER 11

Dear Beatrice

Dear Beatrice,

My earliest memory of you is in your apron baking pies for our family. Although you rarely showed me affection, you'd roll up scraps of blue-tinted, uncooked pie dough and slip it into my little hands from time to time. For whatever reason, I thought it was delicious. Oddly, your eggs were somehow always blue-tinted too—I never knew why.

Though you were our housekeeper, I'll never hold it against you that you never warmed to me. Closeness was an indulgence that our environment did not afford us. There were so many people vying for your attention, as you took care of us while you were taking care of your own children as well. There was little time for *Baby Phoebe.* She was the inconsequential, invisible one.

In 1968, my grandfather hired you to help alleviate stress, presumably most for my mother. You carried duress in your physical being and an unpleasant expression on your face, constantly. There's no mystery about why you weren't smiling. You were probably engulfed in depression, trying to support a large family with little means, turning your pain into constructive anger, because you needed employment and an income. Although my mother and siblings cared about you, I'm sure it seemed that no one worried themselves about how you felt or considered how deeply you needed our support. You were surrounded by a household of people who, caught up in their own struggle for emotional survival, couldn't really see you, and you were expected to play a maternal role for these same children you couldn't completely understand. I tried to stay out of your way as best I could; still, some of my most important memories involve you.

You were there the day I learned to read. I was in Dad's room in the back of the house, where all of the books were, and you were in the kitchen, making food that I neither saw nor ate. I knew that I would be undisturbed as long as I stayed back in his bedroom, so I spent a lot of time there, by myself, spreading books out on his bed, which was chest high to me. I'll never forget the magic of words leaping off the page at me, the first time they organized to make sense, the first time I could conceptualize words. What a world opened up that day while you were standing far away in the kitchen, absorbed in rolling out pie dough on the cutting board on the counter.

I remember that you smoked cigarettes a lot and the sound of your house shoes scuffing the floor when you walked from the front of the house to the back, which was not very often. I also remember when a few of your family members came over, including your daughter—little Abigail—who was my age. We were playing in the backyard with one of my balls, not speaking, just shyly bouncing the ball back and forth. It was one of those bright shiny balls you bought at the supermarket, the ones that were pretty but didn't last all that long.

Suddenly, when Abigail bounced the ball, it hit something sharp and popped. She was distressed, and you became furious with her. I tried to tell you it was okay, but you were already on a tirade of correcting her harshly and insisting that she give me one of her dolls. She had a black doll and a white doll. She gave me the white one. I'd never played with a black doll before. I wondered what it would be like.

I was sad that you made her give up her toy as penance. I didn't want the doll, and I didn't mind that the ball had popped. But my voice was no match for yours, so Abigail and I just looked at each other and conceded. She seemed devastated; it broke my heart. I knew she probably didn't have very many toys, and I was taking something significant. Worse than that, she had also failed at making it a successful visit, just as you had expected her to.

The dolls, like us, had no say over the ways in which they were being separated. It's just the way things were that day in the backyard of our house at Benbrook Boulevard. We kids had a heart for inclusivity, but the world had other plans.

Beatrice, I wish I could ask you about motherhood, and what it felt like for you, taking care of us during such a hostile time. There were so many women who deserved to be asked. The nannies, the mothers, and the grandmothers—like my friend's Nan, who also had ten children but suffered from depression and set herself on fire when she lived in a small Texas town, burning herself alive in front of her children. I suppose you deserved to be asked, too, as did our mother—illuminated and fierce until she burnt out like a stifled star.

• • •

I wonder if you experienced *Twilight Sleep* while birthing your children—a common practice throughout the 1950s that involved drugging birthing mothers with morphine and scopolamine and restraining them like animals, making birthing not *pain free* but *memory free*, while mothers convulsed and hallucinated, as their babies were born struggling to breathe. While most mothers didn't remember the trauma of what they'd experienced, they did miss out on the inherent benefits of bonding with their babies in the moments immediately following birth. By default, their children suffered too.[7]

Maybe things had become more *civilized* by the time you were bearing children, when the medical system had *evolved* into tying mothers down during labor, cutting them open with episiotomies as they were gassed unconscious, and fathers were prohibited from visiting. Back when women were separated from their newborn for an entire twenty-four hours, save the too-short periods of time they were allowed to breastfeed.

Maybe it was only as bad as that: as being told not to ask for your just-born baby... under any circumstances. I'm guessing motherhood, for you, Beatrice, was especially unbearable. You were a mother to your own children, and our family of ten. Where was your safety? Where was your solace? It's devastating to consider such unthinkable practices were imposed on women in places that should have been sacred and safe. I can only imagine. And maybe that's why you were never smiling.

CHAPTER 12

Dear Papa

Dear Papa,

How naïve of me to believe that the troubles in our family started *in my mother's generation.*

You came from a poor family of five brothers and two sisters, born just north of Bowie, Texas, on a produce farm. You formed enduring bonds with your brothers that only deepened when they went on to attend law school and pursue successful careers. There was no stronger family to back your brother, James V. Allred, as he campaigned for his governorship in Texas. Everything about the Allred clan was impressive. You, too, had a penchant for political science and were appointed as the regional administrator for the newly formed Securities and Exchange Commission later in life.[8]

For decades, your family of origin was impenetrable, but it would come to know many trials and tragedies, including the painful and forced separation of your mother and father, though necessary, due to your father's dementia and mental illness, which caused him to believe that your mother was plotting to kill him.

Although your father lived somewhat happily with your brother, James V., during his governorship at the mansion, he longed to be reunited with your mother, but the doctors advised against it. And he came to suspect that others were also out to get him, causing him to sleep with a knife always at the ready. Eventually, although it was a very tough decision for your family, it was necessary for him to be committed to the asylum in Austin, for his safety and the safety of his loved ones.

Meanwhile, your youngest sister, Hazel, was tragically killed by a truck driver who fell asleep at the wheel then crossed into the wrong lane, forcing Hazel and her husband to drive into a concrete bridge pillar. This was only one year after her marriage to W. B. Stokes was hosted at the governor's mansion. After the collision, she died in her husband's arms on the way to the hospital, and your brother, Governor Allred, forgave the trucker, remanded his sentence, then enacted the Texas Safety Association, which increased regulations for trucking companies and no doubt saved future lives.

Just two days after James V. Allred was inaugurated as governor, your youngest brother, Renne, awoke, unable to move, having contracted osteomyelitis of the spine: a life-threatening illness of which he was not supposed to recover. But recover, he did. After nine months of being bedridden in the hospital and dropping to just 90 pounds from 175 pounds, he was healthy enough to be released from the hospital.

You must have been initially very proud of your son, John C. Allred, who was one of the young scientists chosen to gather at a top-secret laboratory in Los Alamos, New Mexico, in April of 1943, to design and build the world's first atomic bomb.

Most of them had been involved in nuclear fission research, but due to secrecy restrictions, few had any sense of the immensity of the project they were about to undertake. The goal in Los Alamos was to leverage the phenomenon of nuclear fission, discovered four years earlier, to produce nuclear weapons in time to affect World War II. A little over two years later, the world would learn that they had succeeded when Hiroshima and Nagasaki were devastated by the most powerful weapons history had ever seen. The war came to a close, and then the Cold War and its nuclear arms race soon broke out on the world stage. Many said that the atomic bomb saved lives in the end, but I still have to wonder how it must have felt for you to know that your son was co-creator of such a weapon of destruction.

You, who served as a sergeant major in the 90th Division of the United States Army from 1917 to 1919, must have seen some value in preventing greater casualties than the bomb itself might eventually produce. I presume, anyway.

I think you were proud of Mama, too, initially. She did well for herself at the beginning and knew how to manage her public self, her public projects, successfully. Rumor has it that you were close to her, and Cita, my grandmother, was close to John C. I'm guessing your dad's mental illness and mistreatment of your mother may have made you all the more sensitive to what Mama eventually experienced through her own challenges.

And so, the cycle continued. Your daughter's death preceded your own by four years—hers in 1972 and yours in 1976. She was not buried in Fort Worth, as you were, but her spirit lives on there at Benbrook Boulevard, at the Lubbock house, and at your home on Simondale in Fort Worth—where she once held us kids captive upstairs, barricading the doors to keep the police from retrieving us to return to Dad.

Where were you on that evening? I don't know, but I am sure that this kind of attention and activity was contrary to the reputation you had established for yourself. I don't think people were as sympathetic, somehow, to Mama's mental illness as they were when your father suffered the same in the governor's mansion. No, Mama could never get off that easily, or redeem herself, after bringing shame on the Allred family.

Photo of Mama; her brother, John C.; and her mother, Cita

CHAPTER 13

Dear Kate

Dear Kate,

We saw you a lot growing up, certainly more than the rest of our older siblings. You were a young adult then—probably around twenty-six years old when you'd returned to us from Canada. We Three Popes were enrolled at McLean Middle School and were grateful for you to bring a sense of wonder into our confusing, preteen years.

You became a mother at a young age—*too young*. Like Mama, you were pregnant at seventeen, with Mark Lins' baby. I wonder what that was like for you. Imagine, after losing Mama, you left to live in Canada, in a literal goat shed, to raise your three boys, a young girl turned mother, on her own, virtually all alone in the world. Looking back now, it must have felt like a desperate measure—and terribly cold, in every possible sense.

During those early years, you sewed clothing for your children; your greatest masterpiece was two immaculate suits for the boys, made with navy and burgundy velvet. I've wondered who taught you this skill. Mama, most likely. I've delved into many of the arts, but never sewing. And while most have come easily to me, I often marveled that you and Steph naturally took to making complicated pieces that turned out perfectly, and you never used patterns at all.

Like the suits and miniature fabric dolls you sewed for your boys and the tiny purse that Steph made—complete with rivets, leather, and beautifully patterned fabric. You both had remarkable talent. I have often wondered if I do, too, if it would come to life once I picked up a needle.

I've also pondered, all these many years, exactly what drove you to leave home to live under such extreme circumstances. The draft, I'm sure, and certainly the pain of losing Mama. You were just a kid, seventeen, doing very adult things. Sometimes it seemed as if Mother's death was hardest of all on you. Maybe you saw it all more completely than we did, through your young adult eyes, while the rest of us were small, and it was just *too much* to bear.

You seemed to be the Harris child who was closest to Mama, though, in truth, finding favor with everyone seemed easy for you. You always had a *light* way of being, as if you did not live through what the rest of us did. Or maybe the lightness was *because* you could not live through what the rest of us did.

It seemed in some ways that you had the most wholesome, unfractured upbringing. I remember you telling me about the time you spent with Papa and Cita as a child; about the pony you owned when you were young, when money must not have been a concern; and about winning tickets to see the Beatles as a teenager. Things had changed so much between the time you were born, in 1952, and when I was born, in 1967. When you talked about your childhood, it felt as if we lived in different families, different universes even.

Your placement among the siblings seemed fortuitous as well. You were most likely adored by Patricia and Johnny as a new little sister. Patricia was six years older than you, so she did not feel as if you were competing for the same resources, and I'm sure she set a good older sister example that Johnny would have been inclined to follow. You were also the oldest of the Harris siblings—you had the cat by the tail and the others looked up to you. You were in charge and you knew it.

I sometimes wondered why you seemed to fall farthest as a result of Mother's death, then I understood. It was precisely that *you had the farthest to fall.* Because you had known the magical, happy times of the 1950s, Mama's death and the reality that followed were likely all the more tragic to you. Maybe there's something to the idea that we Popes grew up expecting less; maybe our poverty mindset protected us, maybe we were saved by only knowing lack.

The hole created by her absence might have served us differently because we were never ripped from a stable, well-rounded world, as you had been. We were jaded from the start and exhausted by our family's tragedies throughout the 1960s—we Three Popes had only ever really known what it looked like to live *without.*

• • •

Yes, you easily found the favor of others. You were strong, had a bit of an armor around you in that you were not one to take on worries unnecessarily. You were the eternal flower child—a true hippie who lived more freely than anyone else—and you were popular with your friends because of it.

The social pressure of the '60s led you to *drop out, tune in,* and *turn on.* Like most of your generation, those beliefs influenced your decision to flee the United States during the Vietnam draft. This mantra also set the stage for how you would handle stressors later in your life.

In truth, I didn't vibe with the *hippie* lifestyle as a kid; something about the practices and energy of it made me feel unstable and insecure. But I appreciated that you would always extend an invitation to us kids, even if I found the activities strange.

Like the time we were all going to sleep upstairs on pallets when you were visiting. You let us know that clothes weren't necessary. I guess everyone loved getting naked in the '60s; they wanted to be naturalists, to feel uninhibited. I was too young to grasp this, so when this option was offered, I just thought it was weird and gross. *I was outta there!*

You never wanted for much in the friends department. People were quick to seek your company, including those at your twentieth high school reunion, which I attended with you. I'm sure I dressed up a little for the occasion, but later realized it wasn't necessary when you showed up in your T-shirt and jeans. No makeup. No bra.

And your friends, now accomplished persons, wanted nothing more than to be around your magnetic personality, still, after all these years, swirling around Kate, who had power, because she neither conformed nor cared. Still.

Dad always said you were the most intelligent. I'm just sorry that somehow you Harris kids did not necessarily see yourselves that way. Especially because all of you were more capable with your hands and living off the land than the rest of us.

• • •

I appreciated spending time with you after you returned from Canada and getting to know your kiddos, and I have especially fond memories of the day you took us all to the antique store and bought me a German cuckoo clock. I hung it in the dining room and admired it for years afterward.

Mary and I loved having your girls spend the night with us at 2701 Benbrook Boulevard. Those times felt sweet and secure—all of us crowded into one single twin bed; it didn't matter that we were cramped. We were grateful to be there for each other, to create wholesome and loving memories with the wee ones.

Rebekah is exactly fifteen years younger than me, just as I am fifteen years younger than you. I gave her the rose James Avery ring at her high school graduation that you gave me for my high school graduation. I wanted her to have something memorable from her Aunt Phoebe, wanted her to feel the safety and security and sweetness of *tradition* in a family of independent thinkers that rarely leaned toward *tradition* of any sort.

Yes, you extended yourself a lot to us, as our older sister, when you returned to Fort Worth from Canada. We spent an abundance of time at your mother Mama Harris's house and also at the home you bought on Henderson, which was run-down but an impeccable buy—an icon in the historic district. In the Fort Worth days, you went through incredible trials as a single mom of eventually *seven* kids, especially when Daniel was diagnosed with bone cancer. That's perhaps when some of your coping mechanisms became a little more pronounced.

Somehow, even the freezing cold nights we Three Popes spent babysitting your sleeping babies in your van, while you were inside at the bar grabbing a drink with friends, made us feel less alone than if we'd been home. It didn't seem that out of place to us, especially given what we had lived through with Mama's episodes near the end of her life. You didn't expose us to anything that others weren't exposed to during that era. Today it might be considered *neglectful*, but in the '70s it was simply parenting. It was what everyone did.

It's sobering to think of how lonely you must have felt, but probably didn't allow yourself to feel, in your days as a single mom. I remember stopping by your apartment once as a high schooler. You were a nurse, and on the clock at the hospital, while Daniel was there in the apartment taking care of baby Sarah. I stopped for only a second; I'd had a friend drive me, since I was thirteen and had neither a car nor a license at the time. It was a short moment in time but one that I'll never forget; it still haunts me to this day.

I entered the living room to find Daniel lying on the floor, with a bedpan next to him, throwing up from chemo. Sarah was in her crib, hiccup crying, hot with flushed cheeks, needing a diaper change. It was evident she had been upset for a while and had just about exhausted herself.

I changed Sarah's diaper but couldn't soothe her completely. Daniel tried to make conversation and maintained a brave, smiling face between his vomiting. As I closed the door of your apartment behind me to leave for work as a balloon girl at the Fort Worth Zoo —I was running late—I was sickened at myself for walking out with every step. As with many situations, it felt there was no one to tell, no real place to turn for help; everyone was too busy surviving. So I kept walking and tried to forget. But I never, ever did.

To this day, that is still one of my hardest memories. As well, I still feel the gripping anxiety of sleeping on the bed at your house with your precious children. I was eleven years old, and they were just babies. You'd tuck us all in together and kiss us good night. By early morning, we would all wake up covered in baby pee—cold, soaked, and itchy.

I'm not sure why I wouldn't have suggested, or insisted, on fresh diapers at bedtime. I was accustomed to not asking, not having much personal power. It still bothers me that I didn't speak out more on their behalf. There was a lot working against us—the cold, the lack of money, the filth—but somehow it would help me today to know that I'd advocated for them. Even if it wouldn't have resulted in a resolution.

• • •

Today, Daniel is in jail, arrested for purportedly calling in a bomb threat to a school in Texas. For many in the family, he's hard to relate to anymore. We lost compassion for him over the years, as his behavior worsened, after so many police incidents, and as he slowly transitioned from victim to perpetrator.

I don't harbor ill feelings or water the seeds of my anger toward him. I can handle that he aggressed on me moments before I officiated Travis and Rebekah's wedding in Marfa, when he was angry that his sister Rebekah had not chosen him, *a self-proclaimed pastor*, to perform the ceremony.

The situation was stressful, but I smoothed things over, assuring him that I was being held to a very tight timeline and promising that after ten minutes I would turn the whole ceremony over to him. He believed me but still demonstrated an angry temperament after his reading, stamping his staff and glaring at Elijah and Oliver from the front of the congregation. I continued with the ceremony, praying that he would move into a new phase of his delusion and that we would get through all of the vows before he started up again. I was aware at that moment just how much was riding on me to pull off the ceremony. Luckily, he refrained from acting out, and the wedding was deemed a success by the guests.

However, I was horrified to learn later about the events that had taken place the previous day, while I had been away rehearsing for the ceremony. Daniel had asked Aunt Adria, my younger sister-in-law, if he could drive the boys to the restaurant for a family meal. She agreed, reluctantly, as Daniel had been up late, screeching through the streets of Marfa, turning donuts in the vehicle until midnight. We could feel the swelling rage of his mind by the way the car sounded. I know Adria was sorry she'd said yes to Daniel that day—we all were.

Once Elijah and Oliver were settled in the back seat of Daniel's car, he locked the doors and drove them recklessly, at ninety miles per hour, to an empty field—not to the restaurant, where he had promised to drop them off. Naturally, Aunt Adria was frantic.

Daniel confiscated the boys' cell phones and held them captive in the middle of a distant field, directing them to find military coordinates. Fortunately, though Elijah was only twelve years old, he had his wits about him. He outsmarted forty-one-year-old Daniel, in his state of delusion, by convincing him the coordinates were back at the hotel. It worked, and the boys were able to persuade Daniel to return them to where we were staying safely. We hadn't understood until that weekend just how much his mental health had declined.

During Daniel's last visit to our house the next year, he discovered Elijah, who was home alone, and terrorized him by forcing his way into the backyard and making a scene with the neighbors. In turn, he also terrified our beloved, seven-pound dachshund Lola. As he opened the gate to leave, Lola raced out quickly underfoot, and in a frenzy, she dashed into the street before anyone could catch her and was hit by a car within seconds.

Those memories are hard for us still, but we press on. I will always love *Little Daniel*, the one Mary and I used to babysit and take to Dairy Queen for a Butterfinger Blizzard. I'll choose to remember him as he was in his younger years, when he was charming and full of love, when he was both street-smart *and* innocent.

Sometimes, Kate, when I was in middle school, instead of going to your house with Mary and William, I opted to stay home instead. I felt I couldn't bear the insecurities that engulfed me there. I intuit you understand that, just as we all understand that we are better grandparents than we are parents. Today, your grandchildren adore you—all twelve of them. You are the enchanted and gentle *Nanny Firefly*. Today, the past is the past—*so be it.*

Phoebe, Kate, and Rebekah in Marfa

Nieces, by Kate

CHAPTER 14

Dear Jody

Dear Jody,

As I write this, I grieve your closeted anguish, your path to self-destruction that somehow you did not impose on others.

How sad that you died at sixty years old. By the time you entered the Veterans hospital that week, your fingers were tracing death. You were much closer than anyone could have ever known.

The family gathered from all places and directions to be around you in your severe illness—to support you and show their love. While everyone rushed, the females of the family made it first. You'd always been gentle to us and extended yourself, truly and boundlessly, whenever you had the chance.

Clearly you were suffering, based upon the amount you were drinking, and yet as far as we knew, you never acted out—no displays of anger, violence, or anything of the sort. Just a lot of numbing, trying to still the sadness within.

Oftentimes you broached the subject of Mama's extreme PMS, which had obviously traumatized you, and labeling it as such seemed your way of making sense of all of it. You were sensitive to her and clearly didn't want to repeat her errors: the crazy yelling, fierce tantrums, and emotional outbursts.

You were still smiling and being Jody up until your last night, which is why many didn't believe you were close to the end. When I called Kate and told her I believed you were dying, she listened. The last thing I wanted was to claim that, yet I had to tell. It felt like an inevitable reality as the words left my mouth, and I had great reservations. I didn't want it to materialize. I prayed in the same breath that it wasn't true. But it was, and Kate knew it too.

Afterward, she jumped in her car from many hours away and drove straightaway to see you. And so she reached you, right before *the end.*

Others came too, hoping to prove it wasn't so, remarking that you were still vibrant and alive. You put up a good front, and I said nothing because I didn't want it to be true. Yet after their visit that evening, it was me who had to make the call to your wife, Nancy, and your daughter, Jessica.

"I know it's the middle of the night, but the nurses have said Jody likely will not make it till morning."

I heard pregnant Jessica scream in the background after I delivered this news to her husband, Rick.

The nurses put you on oxygen and kept you *alive* by artificial means, until Nancy and Jessica showed up. But you weren't really there, even though air was being pumped in and out, and there was a tube taped in place to suction the blood that flowed from within you. Nancy had a hard time looking at you and later wished she hadn't.

You found ways of speaking to us after your passing. Like the strange occurrence when the nurse opened your hospital room door —you had been pronounced dead, but she clearly saw something different.

"Good morning, Mr. Harris, you're looking well this morning," she commented. She saw you as alive and vibrant, even though you were immobile, passed, already gone. I personally think she was gifted and saw your new form.

That night, I was making the brochure for your memorial, and the computer and printer were giving me fits. Finally, at 2:00 a.m., when I got the materials to print, the first page came out looking like the American flag, with red and white stripes. It was surreal. I couldn't get it to do it again, so I made sure your son, Josh, got the only copy. It felt like a personal message from you to me, veteran to veteran.

Then there were the stink bugs. They showed up *everywhere*: on the car that Peter rode in, even when traveling fast down the highway on the day of your funeral; then in Mary's purse and in her dog's food bowl; on me when I was leaving hot yoga; and on my arms as I was doing dishes. We knew it was no coincidence that in your last few days on earth, you had asked your daughter, Jessica, if anyone else smelled stink bugs in your hospital room.

I've felt your presence probably more than any other of the *dearly departeds*. They say our personalities in our spiritual forms are much like those when we were human. Seems true for you—all of your messages have been marked with true Jody humor.

• • •

I felt that the message you wanted me to hear the most was your validation of my marriage to Kevin. You and Nancy were the longest wedded in the family, with Kevin and me following a close second. You two had struggled through some hard times, but chose to overcome them and stayed together. You were no stranger to how much a marriage requires but were forever committed to yours. After you died, I felt a deep sense of your affirmation regarding my marriage to Kevin—despite the typical and real ups and downs.

My favorite message of yours followed the two-year anniversary of your death.

Kevin's niece Leah had asked me to perform her wedding—which was April 14, two years to the day after you had passed—just as I had for my niece Rebekah three years earlier. I agreed but recruited Kevin to perform the ceremony with me. I spoke to you a lot that day, asked for your presence and support. I had written the script for the ceremony, making it as meaningful and personal as I could, and we received lots of commendation at the end.

Kevin and I both felt it was a blessing to have honored Leah's wishes. Upon arriving home, we went for a run. Kevin finished before me and found a mangled piece of gold with sparkling stones embedded in it on the street where we lived. It was an odd discovery.

Because we had the day off, we drove it to the jewelers, arriving a few minutes before closing time. We asked if the gems were diamonds. They were. And the generally disgruntled owner suggested that we *make it into a shank*. Not knowing what that was, I agreed, and told him to make it into whatever he thought was best—*surprise me!*

Before nine the next morning, the jeweler called and said, "Your ring is ready." I was flummoxed and went to pick it up. My mouth fell open when I realized it matched my own wedding ring perfectly. I snapped a picture and texted it to Kevin, laughing and emphasizing the irony that the last text I'd sent Kevin, asking him to call me, read:

Give me a ring, please.

I'm guessing you helped with that one, Jody. Thanks for the gift, brother. When times are hard, I think of your message and relax into the spiritual truth that my life and marriage are divinely affirmed. I know you've got my back just as much as you did when you were here on earth, and I am grateful that you are still teaching me how to live and love well.

Jody in his Navy days, holding a wee one

CHAPTER 15

Dear Peter

Dear Peter,

This may be the most important letter that I write.

Because I have, at times, judged you most, I must be all the more diligent to extend grace to you, to understand that you were a product of experiences that I never witnessed, that you were formed mightily by Joe Harris—the antithesis of a loving, caring guardian.

I know he was your greatest violator. For this reason, and due to other dynamics in the family, it is rumored that you have had the most to overcome. Being born an entire decade later, I was not there to witness it. I have decided when it comes to the past it is best for me not to judge, question, or discern another's truth.

As you have healed, you have been forced to consider the thin line between victimhood and villainy. Like all of us, you have chosen where you stand. Within each of us, there is a spectrum of light to darkness. I pray, my brother, that you remember, especially in your pain, the option to move always toward the light.

I was glad to witness, in your more recent years, the happiness you found with Kwalimu. I'll be forever grateful that the two of you fell in love; that your love redeemed each other; and that in your later years, after your divorce, you sought each other's forgiveness.

I witnessed that your years with Kwalimu were good and productive, with you both working at the Edelweiss Ski Resort in Taos. You were the maintenance supervisor, and Kwalimu oversaw guest services. You both were well-known around town and well-liked as a couple. For fun, you frequented the beauty hot spots of Taos's irresistible geography.

You both traveled to see us a few times in Texas, and you seemed lighter. It gave me hope that you'd made it to the other side of your pain, that you'd finally climbed through the dark valley of your father's shadow.

On those visits, I mostly laughed with Kwalimu. It was hard not to adore her; she was sassy, bright, and powerful. I could see why you were drawn to her and how the power of her spirit made you come awake.

I wish you could have stayed with her; I wish you both could have stayed in the light. It was a powerful place for your love, and it brought all of us joy. Never did two people laugh more together, which was contagious for the rest of us.

Growing up, you were nine years older than me—the brother I wanted to look up to. I remember one of our arguments at Benbrook Boulevard when I was a teenager. I told you that you were *nothing but a drunk*. You told me that I would end up just like you. In that moment, I walked to the sink and poured out my beer and vowed *absolutely not*. Your words made me realize there was a choice, and in that moment, I claimed my destiny. I knew exactly what I couldn't become.

Do you remember when we went to Dairy Queen on the Bluebonnet Circle? When I left a tip on the table as we were exiting that you went back and stole before the waitstaff could collect it? That was your *sometimes* dance back then: often abruptly going out of your way to retract good intentions. It never ceased, in the moment, to surprise or disappoint. It was a pattern that you learned from someone you should have been able to trust. It made me sad to witness.

The day that the opossums crawled under the house and into Dad's shower marked me for life; it was the day I learned to shut off my trust valve, to turn instinctively and instantaneously away when something was too much. It was also the day I understood the depth of what you had suffered.

I opened the door and studied the two opossums, nestled together in the half-finished shower that had an opening to the backyard—and they were still only playing dead. Within seconds, before I could process what was happening, you brought out a baseball bat and began swinging. You made a bloody mess of them.

They didn't move. They remained frozen the entire time, allowing you to bash them senselessly as blood spattered all over the walls. They didn't make a sound. I wondered if they were dead in the first place, but there's no way they could have been that lucky.

It was fast, brutal, and bloody. There were no real words before or after, just you swinging the bat and bringing it down again with all of your might—intent on destroying, desecrating, and punishing. I stood there, breathless, numb, and invisible.

I didn't have to ask you, after that, what it was you lost by being your father's son.

And so, I grieve you from a distance, sending my empathy through this letter.

Peter, I see very clearly your loving self in this moment. I have often wondered if you were petitioned before this lifetime, on a soul level, to play Judas for us. I've theorized that maybe you loved us enough to be the force that shaped our world with the often example of what *not to do*, so that we would flee from darkness and make it safely into the light. I pray light over you, Peter, believing all things can be redeemed. You are first and foremost my brother. And so, I am here to remind you now, the choice and power are yours always to turn away from the dark, to turn toward the light.

On the other side of eternity, I pray your dad finds you, hugs you, and tells you that he loved you enough to play Judas.

I pray next time—you'll get to be the hero.

Peter, Kate, and Steph in more recent years

CHAPTER 16

Dear Steph

Dear Steph,

Never wonder if you have made a difference in this life. You molded me.

You, of all people, have lived with dimension and as a bold example of radical self-compassion. You've learned to live in truth, transparency, beauty, and full accountability of your humanity.

No one could rival the beauty you've created in your art, or the way you live your life, posturing even the dark things to their best use and beauty. Every home you've lived in seems cared for. There is no area of neglect with you. You are a splash of color, expression, and vitality. Your energy envelops everyone who meets you.

Besides your visual art landing you in Art Maui, Wayne Dyer discussed, in an off-hand conversation, the possibility of you illustrating one of his books. He was impressed by you before his passing and requested your illuminating work, because there is no one like you. No one can match the irresistible originality of your manner of dress, living spaces, culinary creations, or one-of-a-kind masterpiece cards you gift to those of us fortunate enough to receive them.

The interactions you have with others feel inspired by a higher light than most of us see. You always know the most piercingly authentic thing to say, and people are often better because you bring your truth into conversations.

You've done a great job of staying active and taking care of your physical body, organically: making your own toothpaste, lotions, and tinctures, and working hard to grow exotic plants that are healthful and beneficial to consume on your then-rented two-acre Maui property.

You're not much for exercise classes because you prefer swimming in the Maui waters that would intimidate anyone else—especially someone of your stature. But the big black rocks don't scare you. You've also moved your body a lot in caring for two acres of land, and have stayed flexible with the yoga ring hung from your living room ceiling.

Now you're back in Taos, New Mexico, where you started off when Sam was a baby. You were living on the property, off the land, back then, and were very capable in building an outhouse, making fires, cooking, and surviving through the dangerous cold of Taos winters.

There you met Harlan, fell in love, and went on to have Guthrie, Amos, and Matty after moving to upstate New York. His sister was somewhat famous in the "jingle" industry and she gifted you a house. The two of you made it a vibrant home—it was like looking at a postcard of sorts to see you sitting at the table as a family, making intricate Christmas tree decorations with the kids, cooking German pancakes, and starting conversations that would last a lifetime.

What are the chances that you would later meet Dad's wealthy first wife, Leandra, at a video rental store of all places, and that she would offer you an artist space at her school to create?

I thank you for looking after us little ones when Mama passed. You were industrious in keeping the house clean, cooking for us, and getting us ready for school. I appreciate your efforts, especially now as a parent, even though I didn't understand then your unrelatable habits of sleeping in or talking on the phone a lot as a teenager.

You'll probably find it funny that it always grossed me out that you wanted to share a glass of banana milkshake while you were reading *Charlotte's Web* to us. For some reason, the idea of sharing your mouth germs didn't sit with me as a little one. At the time, I never seemed to have an appetite because I always had an uneasy stomach, so I would often hide food behind the furniture, which you found. The thought of sharing spit with an older sibling, whose mouth somehow didn't seem as clean as my young one, made it even more uneasy.

I remember you made a lot of peanut butter cookies, never using a measuring utensil, just eyeing the ingredients and always using molasses instead of sugar. I never had an appetite for those cookies back then, but it still comforted me that you made them for us.

You ended up leaving New York—and Harlan—after attending your high school reunion. Something in you just had to get out of the life you'd made; you were like Mama in that way, struggling to break free for your own sanity. It was hard on everyone, but you felt that there wasn't a choice; you were coming out of your skin, suffocating in ways we didn't understand, and insisted we just had to trust you.

You've since been accountable about dealing with the residual anger of your kids. You hold space for them and accept their painful feelings toward you for leaving. Their walk through parenthood has given them a new understanding of who you were and why you did what you did—it's helped your relationships reach a neutral space of human understanding.

Thanks for the lessons in being true to yourself, and thank you for your endless grace. You have taught me that we get back what we give tenfold. I see you doing your best to stay on the high road at every turn, turning off judgment toward others. It's been edifying to witness. Your life is a demonstration that the extension of love and forgiveness is always the best energy; because of you, I heal myself by offering my best to others.

Seeing Stephanie's Maui Space for the first time

A depiction of the Divine Mother by Steph

CHAPTER 17

Dear Ben

Dear Ben,

The world is different without you in it. I now believe that your well-intentioned medications were likely responsible for the suffering in your adult life. Highly sensitive since birth, you'd always been prone to temper tantrums but seemed to outgrow them once you left elementary school.

Only after your overdose, when you were a TCU student, did you begin hearing voices in your head. Their initial whispers became louder and more confusing with the *help* of medication. Still, you pursued contentment as a discipline; you taught us to do the same.

You were a person consumed with the desire to be *good*. You were plagued by your own shadow and the pain in our family, which made you determined to transcend darkness. You were roughly five years older than us and were intentional about preserving our bond by coming to see us at your former home on Benbrook Boulevard, after you moved back in with Jimmy and Joe Harris.

You'd visit us on Thursdays and over the weekend. When you were in middle school, you'd play chase with us, and of course we never caught you. In your high school years, you took us swimming.

On several occasions you came with your girlfriend, Janet, to help us put the kitchen in order, which was an almost impossible job after so many years of neglect. Together, we scrubbed and cleaned for hours. We young ones were both impressed and uncomfortable with your willingness to stay for so long, to take on a task that did not quite seem within reach.

Only years before, you had been one of us. After you left our home and the house deteriorated more, we felt self-conscious about you coming to visit, knowing that you no longer belonged. But your desire to help always rang truer than the distance between us.

We admired how you had integrated into the world with fashionable clothes, a gently used car, being clean, and mastering the power of owning your own schedule. You were our bridge into the future that we aspired to one day reach. We'd set our sights on climbing out of poverty and seeing you made us believe we could—you were proof that it was possible. You were confident, well-liked, successful, and embraced in your circles.

Throughout high school, you were a disciplined student, made straight As, and earned a four-year academic scholarship to TCU. You were handsome, bright, and kind—crushed on by all the girls at school, though you only had eyes for Janet, and the two of you went everywhere together. You two were a handsome couple: your dark brown, stylish shaggy hair and dark eyes were a great match for her light brown hair, green eyes, and tan skin. It was easy to see why you were named class favorites.

On the weekends in high school, you would put on your corduroys and oxfords and go to church. You'd plan all week to pick up

Janet, then swing by Benbrook Boulevard to collect us kids. I wore my best clothes—I only had a few outfits that were church ready—and when Mary, William, and I would buckle ourselves into the back seat of your car, we felt excited and willing to be part of the world that you had found—the world of Janet's family and the Mormon Church, the world that wanted us to be part of it too.

• • •

We were only your half-siblings, but you had a way of making sure every one of us felt valid, seen, and heard. You always remembered us when we felt the least memorable—a common emotion for us Three Popes, born at the end of the line. Though we were only your younger half-siblings, you were devoted to loving us wholly, and we thought the world of you.

Janet loved you, too, for as long as she could. She'd been your high school sweetheart, but as a devout Mormon she felt it best to eventually leave you for the faith she'd been committed to since birth, though you loved her religiously, and she was the only one you wanted to be faithful to. When she broke up with you, the agony was too overwhelming.

You were losing the most important woman in your life—again. So the multiple hits of purple microdot acid were a way to stop the pain. Except that they didn't kill you; they just took you away forever.

Despite your suffering from the overdose, worsened by the many medications you were on as you sought help, you never once said to me what I assumed you felt:

I'm so angry that I did this to myself, that my life turned out this way.

Instead, you continued putting one foot in front of the other—always choosing to remain present, always reaching for the spiritual high road, always studying the practices of spiritual discipline as a most graceful means of transgressing the current difficult moment, as though you had a premonition that your days were limited.

You were one of my great teachers. You showed me how to sit face to face with suffering rather than run from it; to not lose touch with faith, even in the dark night; to honor rightness and justness and traditions that are worthy; to build my life upon the pillars of integrity and dependability.

Somehow, in the later decades of your life, you, Mary, and I seemed to create an unspoken contract to value decency; we arrived there, to a space among us where there were no disappointments, let-downs, or flake-outs. We were committed to keeping even the smallest of promises; we had to, to change the legacy of what we all had lived through.

You came to symbolize intrinsic beauty. The more your physical body aged and failed, the more attractive you appeared. As your soul matured, you epitomized the naked magnificence of the human spirit. Within the reality of a life in which not much was able to manifest due to poverty and your dependent state, you would not forsake your values, or your aspiration to be like the Hare Krishna bird, *to experience happiness through others' happiness.*

You once told me that you were sorry for taking money from the government, and that you were sorry for others that took it too, because you said it felt like you were saying that the small pension was all that you were worth. *Wow.*

And you did as best you could, struggling always with the voices that were often made worse by a change in medicine, or a heightened dose, and you learned to live as an observer of your own mind. When you heard of Jody's death, I already knew that you would never be able to rationalize your existence if the world proved to be too much for him, and so you were gone, with a recreational drug overdose, just seven months later.

I'll never forget hearing the news of your death. It was just a few days after Thanksgiving—the day that I had written one single, special prayer, with you in mind, for those who were celebrating alone.

It was also the day after Kate's son, Daniel, had let our dog Lola out of the yard, causing her to be hit by a car. The pain was excruciating, and the kids were devastated.

Though I knew better, I asked the man who had given us Lola where she came from so that we could get another pup.

I picked the kids up from school early that day—they were feeling especially tender—and we took a long drive to find Lola's breeder to see if she might have another addition for us.

As we were driving, a call came in from a Taos number. I didn't answer, but when no message was left, I suddenly knew.

I made an excuse to the kids about needing to step out of the car. We pulled over; I got out of the vehicle and dialed the number. I froze as I received the news. I was not able to fully process what I was being told. In a haze, I climbed back in the driver's seat and resumed our trip. I stayed quiet. There was no way I was going to tell the kids. It would have been too much on top of losing Lola.

So we continued our trip to the breeder's house, several hours away, and brought home the last pup she had. It was an adorable white piebald dachshund. I suggested we name it Ben.

• • •

Since your death, I've had no choice but to carry out your legacy. I cannot unknow the truths you taught me. I cannot quiet the desire to be the good that I witnessed you to be, to extend to the world the grace you generously demonstrated, even in your worst moments.

You inspired me to keep creating through your songs, which found me again in the days after your death, after years of being buried in the cabinets in the garage. My hands trembled with a reverent fear when I discovered them. I was worried that I would feel *too much* at hearing your voice singing the familiar words you'd written.

Having no cassette player outside of my car, I took a drive. As the tape took a moment to play, I prayed that it would work. And then . . . you were with me.

First, you sang a song called "Alleluia." I didn't remember you singing it before, and as I listened, tears streamed down my face in honor of something greater than myself, in honor of you.

After the song ended, I flipped the tape over, looking for more songs, and was surprised to hear "Alleluia" play again. At first, I was confused as to why the songs recorded on the other side were not playing, but then somehow, I understood—it was *you* describing to me your new reality: *Alleluia.*

And finally, I heard one of your best songs:

Chilly on the Street These Days

Chilly on the street these days,
Not the weather;

Cold stares keep crossing each other—
Who's best at pretending? No one it seems.

Big cars with heartless drivers;
Don't care to see that poor man dying,
Oh yes, he's dying…

Chilly in the home these days,
Not the heater;

Cold families fighting each other,
When will they learn that love is the way?

Big cars with heartless drivers—
Don't care to see that poor man dying,
Oh yes, he's dying.

Chilly in the world these days—
It's the system.

Cold nations fighting each other,
When will they see that peace is the way?

Big planes with heartless pilots;
Don't care to see this earth they're bombing,
Oh yes, they're bombing.

Big planes with heartless pilots;
Don't care to see those men they're killing,
Oh yes, they're killing.

Living hurt for you, Ben. Still, you celebrated; even through your holy lamentations, you sang songs of hope. We both agreed that *if you must grieve, grieve well, and smile into your sadness.* Each moment of your grappling with how to *be* in this world stole your energy, but you struggled on until your final days, and you kept singing, even after death, about your new glorious reality.

Godspede, sweet brother. St. Christopher protects you, here and forever.

Ben

Watching your descent into madness
Was worse than the witness of your death.

Somehow your choosing, through drugs,
To leave all your better parts behind,
Made the why *and* what *of that much harder*
Than if you'd been snuffed out suddenly.

A tragedy but still maintaining
Your finest qualities to the end.

The hardest is that you chose to leave.
That you committed an act without reprieve,
That was final
With no eventuality, no possibilities of turning back.

And ever since, the voices in your head
Plague you with their presence
And plague the rest of us with the tragedy of you.

Gone is handsome Ben;
Gone is the kindest of the kind,
The strong one, or so we thought;
Looked up to by others,

Caretaker of his younger siblings,
Admired by peers.

Trapped in between two families, two fathers,
Somehow you fell in between the cracks
And were never known in the way that you deserved to be.

A fiancé who left, just as your mother did
When she took her own life.
The nine-year-old boy, then and now,

Could not, would not, survive this loss—
Not again.

You amaze me still,
But in different ways,
Your pure heart remains unchanged.
You have persevered in ways that others cannot imagine,

Showing your faithfulness,
To the depressing realities of poverty, a foot ulcer,
Loneliness, and schizophrenia.

Somehow you have found the Zen in being bipolar;

In the inconsistencies and agonizing illusions,
You have made your way to a certain stable truth.

One day, sweet Ben, I know you will find your mother's
arms again.
And you will feel at peace, to feel loved, to feel secure,
to not struggle, to not be alone.

Maybe I will be that for you.

Maybe I will be the one to call you into dinner, to ruffle your
hair, and exclaim over something very safe, and very
ordinary, and very comforting, like the redness of your cheeks.

And you will feel in that moment that there is no other place to be and that you are at peace with the world.

No regrets, Ben.
Maybe you can't see it but I see divinity.

Maybe one day.

Phoebe, Elijah, Ben, Mary, Aaron

Portrait of my brother Ben

CHAPTER 18

Dear Three Popes

Dear Three Popes,

As y'all know, in first grade it was decided by my teachers that I should skip second grade and join the *twin Popes* in third grade. This transition put us alongside each other. Because our teachers were always out to minimize competition between the two of you, and also between Mary and me, William and I ended up in the same classroom.

There was always a sense of pride among us that all of Mama's kids had been coincidentally taught by Mrs. Mayes in the first grade—save William who was put in Mrs. Hughes' classroom.

Mrs. Mayes would often pick me, favored as *the last Pope*, to read in front of class, primarily because I was the only one who knew how to read fluidly.

Remember how from third grade on, we Three Popes would receive *every* prize on Awards Day at Bluebonnet Elementary? Throughout the year, we maintained high standards in the classroom, because it's who we were—there was really no other expression; we also spent our energy participating in class as much as possible. They would call us in alphabetical order: Mary, Phoebe, William.

During standardized testing day, we usually made the ninety-ninth percentile on the Iowa Test of Basic Skills, or came close anyway. William always beat Mary and me out by a few points. We were avid readers . . . it was our pastime.

One of my early school memories was being surprised when I won first prize in a citywide art contest as a kindergarten student. I'd painted a pig, but had long forgotten about it, not knowing that my teacher intended to submit it to the contest. Months later, when I got the pig painting back, there was a big blue ribbon on it. Somehow, in my young mind, it seemed that the ribbon belonged to the pig, rather than to me. I felt proud of the pig for winning the ribbon—not unlike the way Fern felt about Wilbur in *Charlotte's Web*. Because of my happiness for the pig, it was one of the most esteemed moments of my artistic career.

I've had a relationship with art ever since I could remember—we all did. In fact, Will's art eventually landed on the cover of Southwest Art magazine, and he eventually sold canvases for up to $12,000 apiece. But growing up, our creativity was due in part to who our parents were—we never chose it; it was ingrained in us.

Later, as a freshman in high school, I took art with Mrs. Brown, who was married to the assistant director of the Fort Worth Zoo, where Dad worked as an artist. When I made a painting of a tiny rabbit, she shared with me that it was permanently on display on her piano at home—although I scarcely remember doing it and found it odd that she kept it without asking. I also did an intricate wax white tiger on canvas that I gifted to our nephew Daniel when we found out he had bone cancer.

Not surprisingly, we were good readers and writers because Dad modeled this for us. He always credited Mary with teaching me to read—when she did, it came to me rather easily. He'd often recount that when I was three, I would bring him a copy of Kipling's *Just So Stories* and explain to him what they were about. It was as though I could synthesize the information.

Later in life I learned about *sight words* and how little ones study pictures for clues. If they've heard a word while seeing it, the word is comprehended even if they don't understand the alphabet.

Once, while sitting alone in Dad's room, I began studying a book all by myself—and noted that suddenly, the meaning of certain words just leaped off the page and made sense. It was a thrilling moment. That is when I started building my relationship with language.

We Three Popes were also drawn to music and took guitar lessons together. Even more than the guitar, I loved the clarinet and held second chair out of seventeen clarinetists during my eighth grade year. My instrument was made up of parts from four different horns; Dad had bought it in a hockshop. Nevertheless, it worked for me and had a beautiful tone. In eighth grade, Tracy Ward and I performed the clarinet solo, standing during the citywide band competition in which we placed first. She was big and mannish, had dandruff, and had enough Native American heritage that her family received a monthly federal stipend, which was the first time that I had ever heard about anyone taking money from the government. I wondered about the money part—knowing that her clarinet was brand new and that she had been taking private clarinet lessons for years.

When I mentioned to Dad that the Wards were receiving money for being Native American, he told me he'd personally refused Social Security benefits for Mama's death because he didn't believe it was right to benefit from her passing. We children received a small, fixed amount that we used for guitar lessons until the money was gone. During our stint with our music teacher, Dave, we got good enough to play *Eres Tu* as a trio for the Spanish summer festival.

Our endeavors kept us bound together. We chose to primarily spend time with each other and every day walked three miles home, side by side, carrying our books and instruments. Mary and I were especially close; we used to sit at the dinner table and play games or write notes to each other even though we had often spent all day together at school. When we were around nine or ten, Mary and I would take baths together in the winter, which was uncomfortable due to not having heat or hot water. Nevertheless, we made a game of it by sudsing up, then taking turns to see who would be first to plunge into the icy cold water and rinse off. We made a game out of difficult times, a strategy that I still practice today.

In sixth grade, William developed a crush and got his first girlfriend, Diane Creagh. He stopped walking home with Mary and me, and we felt betrayed, but that still didn't keep us from being protective of him if he encountered opposition at school. We always had each other's backs—for better and for worse.

Elementary and middle school were wholesome for us Popes. Though we were poor, we were respected by our friends and teachers; in the classroom we felt valued for our input.

In fifth grade, William and I were part of a group of students who were pulled out of the classroom to work on a special project—a newsletter with the resource teacher, Mrs. Robinson. Though William and I were both smart, we had varying levels of expression. While I wrote fables about a pony named Ladd, created crossword puzzles, and designed step-by-step instructions for *how to draw a puppy*, William wrote a scary but brilliant adult piece called *We're in the House and on the Way.* I had no idea where he got the ideas or material to work from. Somehow, those things were not in my consciousness; he was in another dimension of expression and intelligence.

Mary and I always played it safe as kids; William didn't. He had already lost too much and sometimes seemed drawn to the lure of the forbidden. He was intelligent and simply became bored easily with anything predictable. This all came to a head when he turned five and called our housekeeper Beatrice a *Black B@#%!* Mary and I were shocked. I'm not sure where he'd ever learned the expression. In those moments, it seemed like we had been raised in different households.

When we were little, William enjoyed teasing us mercilessly… and finally I struck back. One day he was bored and pinned me down. He hovered over me—taunting me with his face only inches from mine. I was little then—much smaller than him. I hit him for the first time, and then burst into tears.

In my later years, I put my guilt aside, and we started getting into knock-down-drag-outs on Benbrook Boulevard. That's when I learned to hold my own; I'd even take my shirt off to fight him—that is, until I started looking more like a girl than a boy.

William was capable of some heavy-duty torturing. Once, when Mary was asleep, he duct-taped a god-awful pinching squeaking tree bug inside of her hand. She awoke screaming, unable to get the tape off. Mary never fought back; she just cried. I would have handled it much differently if he had done that to me—and it would have involved fists.

In those early years, I knew that I had to fight back, and not just so William would stop teasing me. It was actually because, in a trio, there is always one odd man out—an extra electron that has no one to pair with. We three were all in constant competition with each other to never be the extra electron, to never be the one to endure extra suffering by being left out or ostracized.

There were plenty of times when Mary and I ganged up on William as well. In fifth grade, he stepped on a nail in our alley. Days later, he swore that he was in terrible pain and that his toe was moving by itself. We were used to his exaggerations and sometimes downright manipulations of the truth, so we had no mercy and called him a liar and a faker. Not long afterward, he ended up in the hospital with tetanus, and a priest administered last rites. Much later we learned that, at the time, tetanus patients only have a fifty-fifty chance of recovering, and we felt sufficiently guilty—truly terrible—for a very long time.[9]

Mary and I didn't fight often. Our most prominent fight was when we were little, and in a moment of me being uncharacteristically angry with her, I threw a metal pencil sharpener down hard on the bed. When it bounced up, it hit her in the face, and I was horrified that I'd made her bleed. She sensed that I was already undone by my guilt, so she seized the moment to yell,

"I'm telling Dad!"

Small and scared, I ran outside and hid in an old, unused armoire in the garage. I stayed there for hours as the three of them combed the neighborhood looking for me. They were panicked. It was out of character for me to hide, and they knew that I would *never* cross the street alone. The longer I hid, the more I worried I'd be in trouble when they found me. So I burrowed deeper into a little ball until finally William located me. He opened the door to the armoire, saw my face, then slammed it closed again.

"She's in there!" he yelled out.

The next time the door opened, Dad's face looked in at me, and I gave a startled scream. Saying little, he scooped me up and hugged me tightly, saying,

"Oh, my goodness! I thought I'd lost you!"

Uncomfortable with being the center of such attention, I was wordless in Dad's arms. I didn't know what to say... so I just said nothing at all.

In middle school, we Three Popes were involved in almost everything: honor society, band, the school paper, the Spanish National Honor Society, and student leadership.

In seventh grade, I was elected president of my homeroom. My teacher observed that I was shy but diligent and took a great interest in me by trying to get me to come out of my shell. In an effort to develop my leadership skills, she put me in charge, during a school event, of introducing a group of visiting acrobats. I trembled as the whole school watched me take center stage—I was scared to death. The group's name was *The Fantastics.* My only job was to say an intro followed by "and they truly *are* fantastic," which sounded so corny to me that it made speaking in front of my peers doubly worse. To my relief I survived, and by the end was even a little proud of myself, maybe even willing to do it again.

During eighth grade, we Three Popes excelled in Spanish, so on our behalf our teacher applied for a scholarship for us to study Spanish in Mexico—an immersion program for one month. Our teacher took care of everything; we only had to pay $50 each.

We were all evaluated once we arrived, and I got put in the highest-level class at the Instituto. Though I was thirteen, I was put in a class with older kids. It got weird when, on the first day, the male instructor wanted to play *spin the bottle* with his students. I assumed it was because there was a very grown-up eighteen-year-old blonde in our group. I chose not to play, but no one noticed. Fortunately, the male instructor did not come back, and I learned a lot from the female teacher that took his place.

In addition to attending school, we stayed with Mexican families who didn't speak English. Some had teenage kids; this meant parties with beer. It was our first exposure to alcohol.

One night, one of our host brothers hailed a taxi for Mary, William, myself, and a girl named Elise to return to our temporary homes. It was raining cats and dogs. That night we learned the scary way that the taxi wasn't actually a taxi—it was just a random white car with a drunk driver inside who'd pulled over when we'd put our arms out to hail him.

On the way home, William, in all of his eighth-grade wisdom, ended up in an argument with the driver about whether Mexico or the US was superior. I couldn't get out of the car fast enough. When we arrived at our hosts' home, Elise and I attempted to get Mary into the house without anyone noticing that she was having trouble standing. Meanwhile, the drunk driver urinated in the street, in the driving rain, and continued arguing with Will.

Suddenly, something whizzed by my right ear and hit the wall. A bullet. Fired by the drunk driver.

Horrified, Mary, Elise, and I hurried into the house, while still trying to maintain the cover of normalcy. Our Mexican mother asked questions, and we assured her that Mary wasn't feeling well. Despite our explanation and careful actions, word of our misbehavior got back to Mrs. Ravel, who was a chaperone staying in another household. Later, she said she would have made us return to the states had she not known our father. Mary and I weren't used to being in trouble. It was weird and unsettling to acknowledge. But it was wrong, and we knew it. Unfortunately, the feeling of mixing alcohol and shame would become more familiar to me during high school.

During my teen years, I lost myself temporarily, as many do. Though I kept my grades up and worked at the Fort Worth Zoo, as a balloon girl, I drank a lot of beer to counter my social discomfort. It seemed I always had a boyfriend too—probably because I wasn't looking for it. To me, it all seemed part of the same escape.

As a junior, I remember winning fourth place in a citywide contest for an essay on individual rights that I wrote in my advanced placement English class. Although I was largely an A student, my English teacher and I got on like oil and water, and for this particular essay, she made me rewrite it more than once and never raised the grade over a B. Finally, when all our work was submitted to the citywide competition, my B paper earned fourth place. But when they called me over the loudspeaker to come receive my award, Mrs. Smith never acknowledged it in class. It was small of her, and we both knew it.

It was a somewhat painful experience—being at odds with a teacher—which was not my norm. I remember feeling worlds away from her, and there seemed to be no bridging the distance. I felt her judgment and disdain and could only respond by moving further away. To me, it seemed that her humor was self-indulgent, naïve, and unrelatable. In turn, I didn't feel inclined toward laughing at her clever little witticisms in class.

That experience alone has made me more sensitive as a coach and mentor to high school students who need to be loved through their confusion, awkwardness, and discomfort. I've learned that sometimes they are not exactly clear on what they're feeling. It's a good time to remind them of the great people they are and to keep criticism at bay.

When I finished high school a semester early—at the age of sixteen—I enrolled in junior college with friend to take advantage of a free semester before graduation. During that time, I also worked full-time as a salesgirl at Cosmopolitan Lady—an upscale, inclusive health club, which was a brand-new concept at the time. I made substantial money and after long work days frequented the bar next door with my co-workers. From my new place in the adult world, I grieved getting out of school early and growing up too fast—and missed Mary and my friends at Paschal High School.

By that time, William had chosen to drop out, which was super painful to witness. Taking our final class photos without him in them devastated me. I tried to reason with him, before he made his final decision, but to no avail, and ultimately, I just kept moving forward, one step ahead of the pain.

This schism with William emphasized what I had always known—the three of us came from the same family but yet didn't come from the same family. For the most part, Mary and I felt close to Dad. William was a bit of a trouble chaser from the very beginning; having been labeled a misbehaver, he'd already decided he *was* one. Through his own suffering, he picked a lot of fights with Mary and me and consequently stayed at odds with Dad during these times. Not unlike how Dad had never earned his father's acceptance, it seemed William struggled to earn Dad's approval too. There was never a question in our minds whether Dad loved him, though.

For the record I want to say that William was never truly errant; he was a good boy who was convinced that he was bad. To this day, he is capable of being more spiritually evolved (when he so chooses) than anyone I know. I pray he makes that choice permanently going forward, for his sake and for the sake of all those around him who will benefit mightily. The world will be better for it, there is no doubt.

During our junior year at Austin College, Mary and I went to Mexico again for an entire month during the January term. The structure was very similar to our eighth grade trip, and we were thrilled to experience the steep learning curve in Spanish and enjoy the beauty of San Miguel de Allende. Later in life, Mary would use this experience as a building block. She continued studying Spanish in her master's program and eventually moved to Mexico for almost a decade—thriving as a dean at a prominent university.

Today, she and her Kurdish husband own a translation company, and Mary is also an AP Spanish teacher and administrator.

While we were in Mexico, we learned through a letter from Dad about zookeeper Mike Bell's tragic death by an Asian elephant. Evidently, he had broken his own rule by moving the elephants single-handedly, and one had knocked him down, crushing his head. I know it must have been traumatizing for Dad to digest the news as he had actually seen Mike's body soon after the accident. We kids were a world away, which made it both better and worse. Years later, I would see an article advertising that Mike's ghost had been repeatedly spotted in front of the cafe at the zoo. It seemed to indicate that his soul was not at rest, and yet, his spirit had opted to continue engaging in the work of his earthly life, a choice that seemed to exhibit peace. I hoped so anyway.

A vivid memory during my college years was working my summer job at The Hop. It was a famous bar in Fort Worth, and the room felt like Texas—complete with neon lights on the walls, antique décor, and a smell of beer and cigarettes that lingered. The regulars became like family; they'd come to talk about their lives for hours and watch the bands play. Though the room was small it was a quaint venue that had hosted some of the greats—including Bob Dylan back in the '60s. Being a dive that drew tourists, it was used by one moviemaker as a filming location for a scene featuring musician Edie Brickell in *Born on the Fourth of July*, a movie about a paralyzed vet played by Tom Cruise. Seeing it on the big screen made the locals feel famous—like the whole world was now in our favorite spot.

During the school year, Mary and I pursued our studies rigorously.

Much like in elementary and high school, our professors were impressed by our intelligence and seemingly identical responses. When we eventually tied for *Outstanding Senior Woman* at Austin College, no one was surprised. An article was put in the local paper about us—we shared the honor of looking practically identical in the black and white photo. As much as I've always felt Mary—I, too, have wondered if we are telepathic. We are certainly connected. Though William didn't attend college with us, he was always close to us in mind and spirit—an integral part to the dynamic trio—*The Three Popes*... who celebrate with each other through the best, grieve through the worst, and hold each other... no matter the circumstance—*forever*.

Documentation on Michael A. Bell's ghost

Zoo Keeper Crushed by 4-Ton Bull Elephant

January 11, 1987

FORT WORTH, Texas (AP)—A 4-ton bull elephant who knocked down a handler and crushed him to death has been isolated for observation, but Fort Worth Zoo officials said they are convinced the animal did not kill deliberately.

Sam, an Asian elephant in his early 20s, knocked senior elephant keeper Michael A. Bell to the ground with his trunk and stepped on the trainer's head as Bell was moving the bull and two female elephants to a larger pen.

Bell's assistant, John Leggett, rushed to his friend's aid, dragging him out of the animal's reach, said police patrolman Bill Chude.

ADVERTISEMENT

"No one actually saw it," Chude said. "They saw the bull standing over him."

Bell, 35, of Fort Worth, who handled elephants during most of his 14-year career, was pronounced dead at the scene Saturday, said Ken Seleske, the zoo's assistant supervisor of education.

There were no signs that any of the elephants were mating or in heat, said Dr. William H. Kirksey, a zoo veterinarian.

"Sam was probably pushing the females around a little bit in a male-female relationship. He was just trying to assert his dominance," Kirksey said.

"We're morally convinced he was acting normal for an elephant," he said. "Once something is down at his feet, it's almost a reflex to either kneel or push the object away where he could see him."

Seleske said it was the first fatal accident in the zoo's 78-year history.

Documentation on Michael A. Bell's death

Sisters share AC 'Outstanding Senior Woman' honor

Phoebe, left, and Mary Pope, sisters' togetherness continues.

Mary and I tied for the Outstanding Senior Woman *honor at Austin College*

Mary and I (right) sit with our sister Kate and high school friend Jon Midglea, enjoying burgers at The Hop

Mary and me in our Brownie uniforms

Photos of me as a baby, taken by my dad

Mama with twins Mary and William and Dad's mother,
Mary Slater Bradford Pope

Will and I have sons seven months apart, who were inseparable when we all lived together in Texas. Elijah is on the left, and Oliver is on the right.

CHAPTER 19

Dear God

Dear God,

We've come a long way together.

I used to think I needed someone's permission to know You fully, that You were something outside of myself and that I needed to be good enough and normal enough to deserve the invitation. At the time I couldn't imagine feeling relaxed in a relationship with You because I only had the awkward, uncomfortable feelings I drew from my few visits to church.

Imagine the glory of the moment when I realized, finally, that You were inside of me the whole time, as close as my breath. For years I couldn't see past the in-your-face energies of the well-intentioned folks who wanted to bring the lost little Pope children to church. They wanted to save us, introduce us to You, and perhaps give themselves a heavenly boost in the process.

I always felt a stranger on those visits to church, sitting on the pews that for some reason made my legs prickle and itch. I didn't understand the price of the ticket or the unspoken inferences of why we were being invited. Perhaps I felt the pressure of being a charity case, as though we were not clean enough to find our own way there.

In their eyes, we were outsiders and flawed because of this. Dad was a man who had not succeeded in being one of them, though they were willing to teach him the right way. We, his children, became part of a secret we weren't in on—we couldn't grasp the nuances. We were forced into the steps of a strange dance—of trying to belong, to believe, to relate. It was an expectation put upon us without our knowing or consent. What were we supposed to think or say?

At times, random adults would surface to volunteer a little too eagerly to collect us on a Sunday from our dilapidated house with the overgrown grass, in clothes that were always a bit off, and transport us to a chapel full of people who would *ooh* and *ahh* over how beautiful we were, while mincing words and secrets that were not entirely over our heads. It created enough anxiety and stress to keep us from bridging the chasm between ourselves and those families, never mind making the spiritual jump.

We just weren't good enough, and we felt it. Not just after Mama died, maybe even before.

How great to realize later, in my adult years, that I had known You from a very young age, that I met You on the floor of my living room while sitting beneath Mama's piano as the chords to *Oh When the Saints Go Marching In* would strike up and make the wooden slats beneath me hum while Mama's voice carried all of us through the air. As the piano swelled, I felt myself encircled by those saints and felt their love encompassing me as we approached the proverbial pearly gates in our dancing march, arm in arm, toward You.

I didn't recognize that it was You—at the time or even later—because that You was nothing like the You that they were pushing me toward at church. But under Mama's piano, I felt a love and a bigness, delivered to me by the music and the joy of singing together, that I knew did not start or stop with me. Under the piano, I found You, in a suspended place where there was neither loneliness nor worry nor absence, and in those moments, I felt the pure power of belief and came to understand what faith could create.

It was a force strong enough to overcome obstacles, to reinvent life, to make things new. It was the power of God within me, the same power that spoke to Moses, revealing *I am that I am*. It was the powerful Christ who strengthens me—whose love is not reserved for the wealthy and unbroken, whose love belongs to everyone—beginning with the little children: we three, tiny, worthy Popes.

So, God, as I inch through the years before I am reunited with Mama, I ask that You do me a favor. Please let her know I cannot wait to see her, that her children look forward to hugging her, that we are coming home soon. Please tell her it will be just like the earlier days, when we would gather around the piano to hear her sing "We'll Be Coming around the Mountain When We Come."

CHAPTER 20

Dear Betty Carter | Dear Straw Man

Dear Straw Man and Betty Carter,

Having just written a letter to God, as I sit down and write a letter to you in unison, I realize that I am, once again, writing a *Dear God* letter.

For better or for worse, you both came into my story, not because God didn't love me, but because He did.

You were both an intrusion into a sacred relationship, and in pushing you away, I also pushed myself closer to my own truth and nearer to God. I should thank you because you were a reason for me to seek Him, a reason to have found myself alone and in need of an answer that only He, in His infinite wisdom, could offer.

Straw Man, shame on you for walking around shirtless, strutting like a peacock with little brain matter, crowding my time with Mama and assuming that I would want a relationship with you in any way. I will never forget the time when I was tiny and you lifted me high above your head, in your lovestruck moment with my mother, searching for God knows what within yourself that was unfulfilled, as you were twenty years her junior.

I remember you that night, your blond and shallow self, lifting me up and asking if you could be my daddy. I was high in the air, suspended, and it seemed as if you were not going to let me down until I answered yes. You told me you wanted to be my father. What you forgot to ask is how I felt. And if you had used even a fraction of that small brain you were given, you would have known the answer to your question before you asked.

That night, you slept on one side of my mother, and I slept on the other. I was filled with the sense of wrong that you were, and my skin crawled to be near you at all. I say to you now what I could not say then: "Put your shirt back on, man, and get out of my mother's bed. Face the fact that you were never in the same league as my father ...that the only chip you had to barter was your sexuality with a woman who had lost her mind."

And Betty Carter, you were the quintessential Gladys Kravitz, as unattractive and unintelligent as the day is long. I don't remember ever having a real conversation with you, just eating insufferable, too-early dinners at the Carter family table with bright afternoon light flooding the table, which was topped with white Wonder Bread and butter. You never seemed to cook, you just opened cans. You sat and said nothing as your husband made perverse comments about your sixteen-year-old daughter's womanly figure, gesturing her hourglass shape in the air as he made *mmm* noises. You cackled weirdly in your horn-rimmed '60s glasses, the same way you laughed with your obese son, John, whom you used to kiss like a lover in front of all of us.

"You didn't last a single pucker!" you'd say to your own son.

None of us ever spoke during these transactions. Our young minds knew it was wrong, but there was no point; the concept of relating with you in any way did not exist. We were speechless that you would be so unaware of yourself and the screamingly obvious unconscious moments that made up your life. We wanted none of it. You ate Wonder Bread while Dad made us sandwiches out of tiny loaves of rye bread, cream cheese, and olives; sometimes there would be liverwurst and Swiss cheese. Even in our poorest moments, we were not Wonder Bread eaters.

After we left, I felt I despised you as a child but now, years later, it's hard for me to wish ill upon you. You got everything you had coming—that's the way spiritual laws work. We are not punished because of our sins, we are punished through them.

You and your husband treated children like sacrificial lambs for your twisted sexual pleasure. We were innocents with our mouths bound—we had no one to tell. Meanwhile, you attempted to destroy Dad's reputation with your projections, a diversion from the fact that you viewed Mary, William, and me as playthings for you and David Carter.

You underestimated William, not banking on him to be the fireplug that he was. He was young but never compliant; when he called you a bitch, believe me, he spoke for all of us.

Dear Straw Man and Betty Carter,

Your shadows taught me to run toward the light inside myself and helped hone my instincts to recognize evil in a second when I see it. In turn, I learned to liberate myself from people like you: to run home, to jump over every fence, to uphold my boundaries, to honor my intuition.

CHAPTER 21

Dear Kevin

Happy thirty-two years of marriage, dear Kevin!

After three decades together, each year deepens my love and appreciation for you; each year brings a new understanding of just what love is. I thank you with all that I am, the girl that I was even before I met you. Our story started that long ago. I remember it as though it were yesterday: meeting at Austin College in the fall of my sophomore year, dating right away. You were funny and bold—and even before we exchanged words, we saw a little of ourselves in each other. Months into the relationship, we were off to a strong start, and yet I got nervous when you said you wanted to visit me in Fort Worth over Christmas break.

I discouraged you, not because I wasn't crazy about you—I was!—but because I was not ready to share my former life and my upbringing with you yet. I didn't want you to visit me in Fort Worth and see our rundown house, the house that literally no one entered after my mother died when I was five. This was true until my teenage years when Will finally invited a friend over—the same friend that went to school the next day and told everyone that Mary and I washed our laundry in the bathtub. It was true.

No, I was not willing to mix my new college world with my high school world. I was not ready to share my upbringing with you, in a rundown house where we grieved Mama's death—where dogs once burrowed in our dresser drawers, where Peter killed the opossums, where we all washed our laundry in the bathtub.

And so, in December of 1985 I told you not to come. But you came anyway. After years of keeping so many people out of our house, my door was closed. It took you to open it, Kevin.

Yes, eventually we had friends visit our house in high school.

In fact, our house became a popular hangout despite its not-so-great condition. As teens, I think our friends loved the "realness" of its disrepair. There were no pretenses, and definitely no air conditioning in the Texas summer heat.

Still, I was not ready for you to see our home. I even broke things off with you because you were so persistent in your pursuit of me—even when I tried to shut you out.

I didn't speak to you over Christmas break to make sure you were discouraged. Nevertheless, you got in your car, drove the 700 plus miles across Texas, and found our street on Benbrook Boulevard, even before Google Maps.

What I loved about you immediately then is what I love so much about you now. When you believe in something, there is just no shaking you loose. You believed in us—from the very start—before I was brave enough. How beautiful is that?

Thinking back to your certainty and determination, I am nothing but grateful. And I just want to say to you, Kevin, thank God you came in through my door. Thank God you did not give up on us but instead, you kept believing. *Semper fidelis*, always faithful.

Connecting the dots today, of course I see God's hand in this relationship that was meant to be, divinely planned long, long ago. I see all of it perfectly now.

And so, I say thank you, Kevin.

My five-year-old self thanks you, my teenage self thanks you, and my fifty-three-year-old self thanks you most of all. Please know forever that I love you completely in the way that God means for a woman to love a man. Nothing left over. I've given it all to you.

And please know that if I did not wake tomorrow (I plan to!), I will have known the most divine love possible. My earthly heart is forever content. No words do justice to the love you have shown me, to what you have given me in your sureness and certainty, from the very start. Trust me, though, I'll keep trying.

Our love is both painfully human and brilliantly divine.

There was no other choice for me.

It was only you.

To Kevin, a Kid Raised in the 70s, Like Me

We Shall Overcome.

We recognized immediately—
Survivors in each other,
It was evident;
In one look, no words spoken.

You asked me later when I first knew.
It was then; we both did.
Before any words were ever spoken.

Does it matter now where your wounds came from?
Or just that we both had them?

We hurt each other a lot.
Because they hurt us a lot.
Guess the buck stops, though.
Has to somewhere.

Tell them I won't leave you behind, won't leave them behind.
I made a promise to our teen selves.
Or do you want me to tell them that we weren't capable,
just couldn't after all?

I had to go off and grow—
But now I'm back,
Wise, not broken.
Now I can finish what we started.

Long ago, he had come in the night, a thief;
Holding my mother's hair, your father's heart.
"What have you done with them?"
And the blood dripped in circles, spatters around my feet,
a sizzle in the fire.

Finding who you were before you were hurt, before you adopted defenses that hurt all of us.
You don't belong to those that hurt you. You belong to us, forever and ever.
I am ripping off my shirt now, tying the cape, stretching arms to fly.

Tell them I'm coming.
I've gone back to find us in the fire.
Tell them it will be my hand that reaches in.

I love your twelve-year-old self just as much.

Tell the children I'm coming.

We shall overcome.

Phoebe and Kevin in Seaside, Florida, 2019

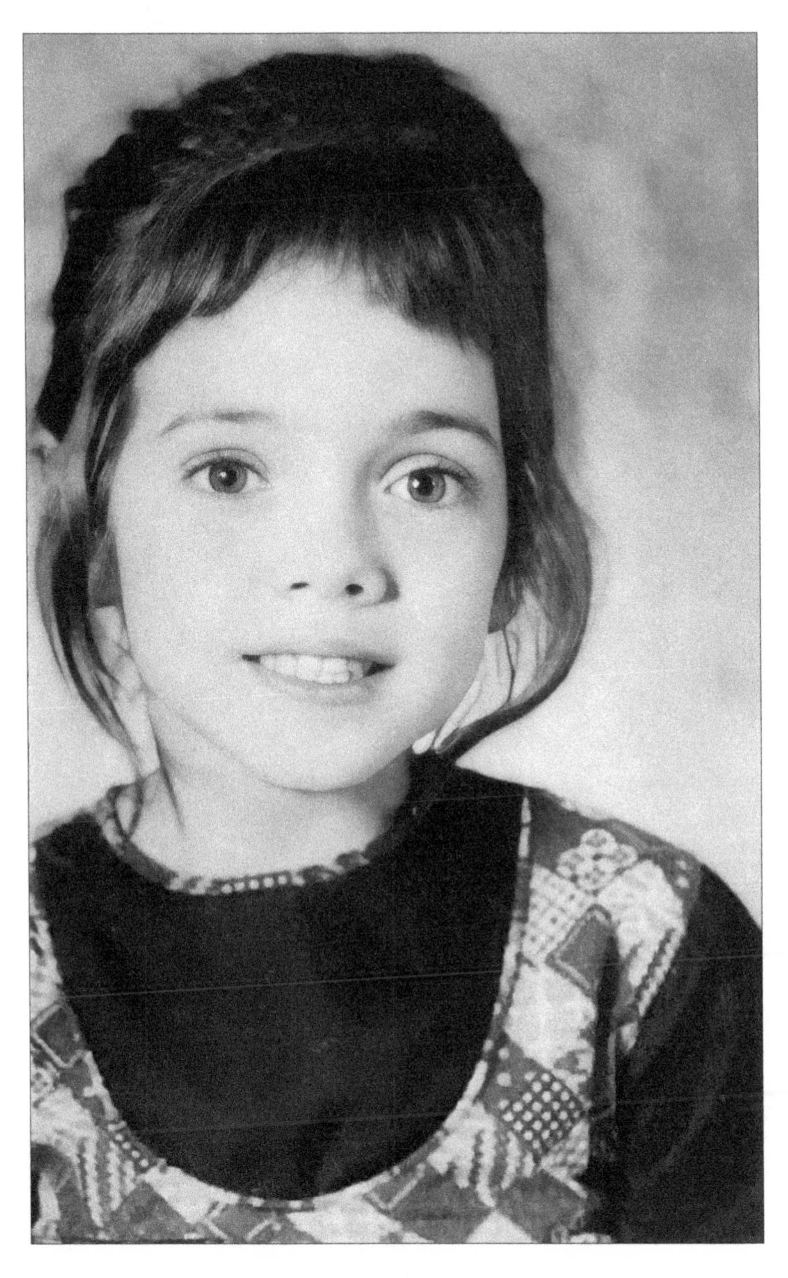

Phoebe, age five

Senior Year, Botanical Gardens, Fort Worth, Texas

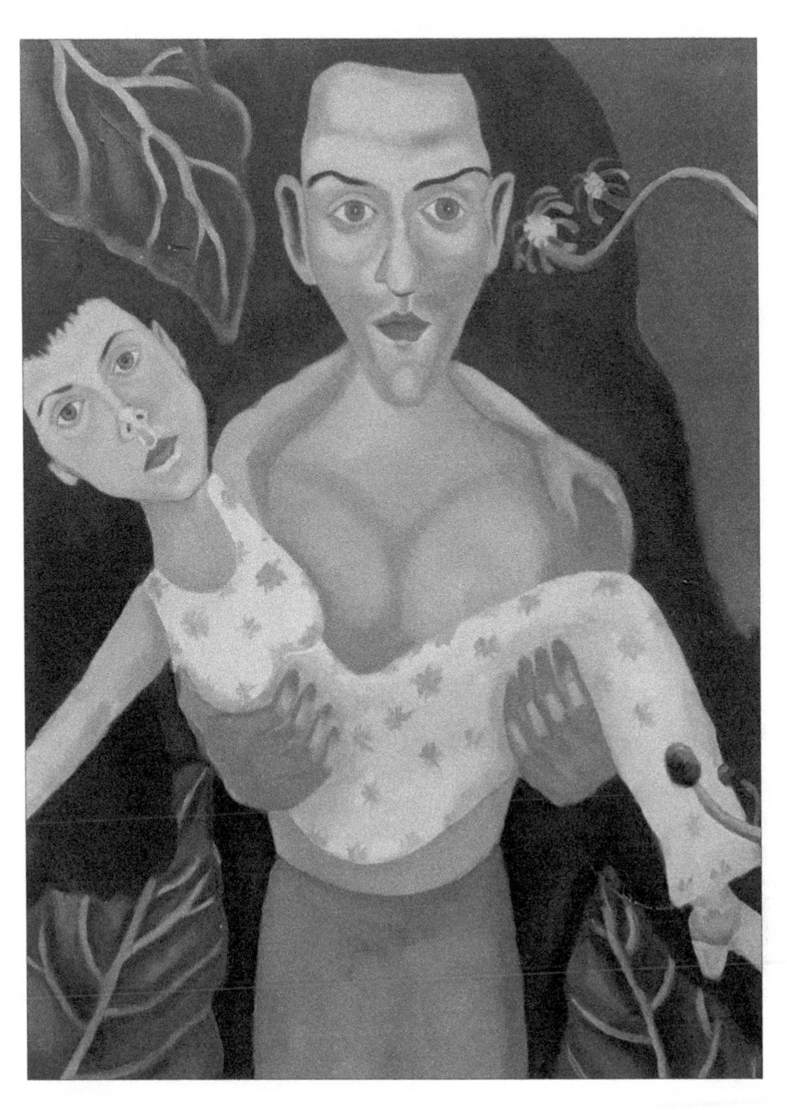

Longing for motherhood

Quick capture of Kevin, 1998

CHAPTER 22

Dear Sisk Family

Dear Sisk Family,

It's not easy merging families. We try our best anyway, despite divorce rates rising above 50 percent.

As I've told many, especially in the context of my own family of origin and in regard to my pastoral counseling studies about marriage and the family, I've stopped using the word *dysfunction* and started using the word *design*.

By considering dysfunction an integral part of the plan, we give God credit for allowing it, knowing it is for our best and is neither accidental nor a collective failure on our part. It is purposeful—it maximizes our spiritual growth and draws us nearer to our creator.

We don't escape it. No families are immune to it. The best we can hope for is to be paired with someone who has been around the proverbial block a few times—spiritually speaking—and is interested in cultivating the fruits of the spirit rather than the fruits of the ego.

When Kevin first told me about his family, he noted that his mom was a clannish Lebanese woman, and that he was *ugly* compared to his two brothers. That's what sticks out in my mind anyway. As it turns out, his mom was open and friendly to me—in no way *clannish*, though definitely prioritizing her own family above all else. Kevin's second comment—his comparison to his brothers—was an unfamiliar dynamic to me, and was perplexing in terms of why it would have ever been spoken in the first place. Neither of these *comment* memories is remarkable in the definition of Kevin's family (in fact he was being a bit flippant when he made them,) and the only real recollection is that his observations seemed categorically different than comments I would have offered about my own family, merely a foreshadowing of our different family dynamics, if you will.

The more I learned about Kevin, the more I compared his family to my own—and I was caught up in comparing my insides to others' outsides. I falsely believed my family was dysfunctional and the Sisk family was the epitome of *normalcy.* It was an inaccurate reading by a young mind who was yet to understand the true nature of God's kingdom.

Like all families perhaps, our two families experienced a similar pressure to present as *normal.* For us, it was from the outside in: through people like Betty Carter putting pressure on Dad and my siblings to teach us how we *should* live. For Kevin, it was an expectation placed upon him by his family, a good upstanding family, who unwittingly curated their reputation in the public eye.

The spectrum of private pain became more visible to both of us as the years went on. As we grew and matured, we understood that we both carried shame (an element that is part of all of our human stories), and although the markers of extremes were different on our spectrums, the pain we experienced was parallel. The concept of divorce was debilitating for Kevin as a young one. In my family, it paled in comparison to my mother's suicide and living in secret. Yet, I believe in many ways our suffering was in equal measure. Our families held different standards for divulgence of the truth. In my family, we brutally called each other out, often too brutally. In Kevin's family, many topics were off-limits for discussion or swept under the rug.

And although family secrets and markers for family norms are different, as ours were, still the necessary path toward growth that unfolds before all of us is the same: to sit in honest, loving examination of our "truth" as adults, in order to sift out false narratives and heal them rather than unwittingly pass them on to our children. Until we grow tired of the patterns of the past that do not serve us, we can neither change nor heal. In every family, something will hurt us—break us. We will struggle with something, and we will become stronger because of it. Families are made up of broken people. We are all on the path together. There is no right or wrong, better or worse—just imperfect human dynamics we are called to overcome.

We all receive what we need to work on in this lifetime, and in turn, I was given a sister-in-law who is my husband's ex-girlfriend. The complications in the beginning were many. Every member of the family had a unique lesson to learn that could only be mastered through their choice of right thought, right action, and right energy. Over time, we have overcome triggers, found resolve, and stepped into lessons of self-worth, trust, respect, integrity, and boundaries.

We have all *learned*. We have stopped repeating old patterns that do not serve us—earning us a win for the combined family.

My greatest hope is that we use our healing powers to see the next generation of our family thrive—to protect MJ, Leah, Elijah, Sarah Katherine, and Ethan from poor habits and curses they could potentially inherit.

I pray they will not be wounded by the wake of us but will be stronger because of our failures that we have had the courage to face; I pray that rather than live in contempt, self-righteousness, arrogance, or self-defense, they will get their emotional needs met and become good communicators and healthy, reciprocal partners to their spouses.

The curse of narcissism has haunted us all; it is woven into the fabric of the extended family, indeed in every family. When Kevin and I came together, we merged histories—mine carrying histrionic female energy and Kevin's carrying arrogant masculine energy. It's poetry, really.

And what is also poetry is that Kevin was raised largely by a very loving single mother, just as I was raised by a very loving single father. And it has occurred to me many times over the years that the likeness of Kevin's mother, Bonnie, and my father, Tim, sets a beautiful foundation for shared values of family, strength, hard work, and decency. And in fact, in my father's final hours, he longed to be at home, in my house, where he passed—and one of his final requests was to partake in a last wonderful meal, cooked by Bonnie, a meal just like the others we have been blessed to share, over and over again, over many years together. And although my father was not able to eat in those final days, we fantasized together about what Bonnie would prepare for him, in the kitchen of my house. And in his altered state of pain medicine, in those final hours, I know that he experienced one last divine meal, his last supper, at the table with the Popes and the Sisks, in deep conversation with Bonnie over the perfection of her fried chicken.

And over the years, it has also been an observation of irony that Kevin's father and my father were polar opposites, in every conceivable way. I have come to appreciate the richness of this, and to understand the balance it has brought to our life equation, just as I have learned to love and appreciate Kevin's father, Martin, for his zany, unconventional, very-present ways.

Yes, we as a people are a dysfunctional *design,* and yet we have learned to function well in embracing God's design, all of us together.

At times, others have commented on our "perfect" family. It's true that it's perfect in its imperfection—just as every family is. But I would like to set the record straight for those who might compare—and feel pain because of it. The spiritual truth is that we have suffered every vulnerability known to the human condition within the context of our extended family. Whether we face ourselves—our own issues—with honor, truth, and love is the standard by which we should be measured, as opposed to the illusion of who others believe us to be.

Our family story, just like all family stories, contains all of the components of suffering, betrayal, forgiveness, enlightenment, and redemption that repeat throughout generations for the sake of our spiritual growth and for the ultimate sake of our spiritual enlightenment. It was set in motion long before us, and we get to decide the length of the story based upon changes that we make to the script. So as we work through this life, striving for vulnerability—coming together and falling apart again—I have to say: it has been an honor to suffer well with you.

Together, we smile into it.

When we have no more triggers, we will know that we have forgiven well and grown into the sacred space that God has prepared for us here on this earth, in preparation for what lies beyond. We will know that we have practiced loving ourselves first as without this practice we cannot eventually learn to love others first, as He does.

We will know, farther along, that all of the challenges, all of the suffering we endured in our sacred earthly contracts together, was not because God doesn't love us, but because He does. And we will realize, farther along, that he paired us with just the teachers we needed to learn our soul lessons. No mistakes in His kingdom. We will realize later how important it will be to turn to one another and say "thank you" for the part we have played in each other's soul growth.

Yes, in the end, we will know that God gave us each just the perfect amount of pain and growth that we uniquely needed to face to become whole again, enough so that we would become strong in real ways of the spirit and would no longer recognize pain as pain. In the end, we will know that He gave us enough to be baptized in fire so that we could rise up, triumphant from the ashes, and that His love was so enduring, He gave us as many chances as we needed to learn our lessons. And so the healing goes.

I am grateful, above all, that my primary soul mate, teacher, and companion is Kevin Sisk, whose name I have adopted, and whose beautiful children have been born out of such a sacred, vulnerable, human union.

Long live the Popes, and long live the Sisks. May each generation heal what is theirs to steward, so that the legacy for those who come after is only love. Let us keep no more secrets, for our secrets become the wounds that our children, and our children's children, must heal.

Long. Live. Love. For all of us.

Commissioning ceremony immediately following graduation

CHAPTER 23

Dear Elijah

Dear Elijah,

I've told you, maybe too many times for your twenty-year-old self, that the days after you were born are some of the happiest of my life. We wanted a baby for so long, and with your arrival, it was as if we went from deeply yearning to deeply fulfilled. It was as if all the boxes got checked overnight. Suddenly we found ourselves in the middle of the most beautiful story ever.

I remember vividly the first newborn nights of your coming ... holding you, feeding you, rocking you, all the while listening to the same beautiful, slow classical music that I played throughout my pregnancy.

Your birth sparked a joy and contentment that I had not experienced before. I remember thinking that if time stood still, and we stayed in that moment forever, I'd be just fine with that. Honestly, I remember wondering, for a second, if it was real.

Prayers brought you to me... I'm sure of that. I thank my sister Mary for leading the prayer circle, all the way from her home in Mexico. After Kevin and I had done all that was humanly possible to have a baby, we quietly submitted to our reality. That is, until my sister Mary called to suggest we form a prayer circle—with some of her friends in Mexico and some of my friends in the US. I was on board. There were five of us total and we spent four days praying for each person. Mary suggested we pray for a baby for me. I agreed but asked to go last, feeling a little bit vulnerable.

The long and short of it is that forty-five days after we started the prayer circle, after women who didn't know each other were praying earnestly for one another for twenty-five days, after eleven years of trying, I found out I was pregnant. It's the reason that my tagline is "I believe in miracles."

Yes, your coming into the world was so transformative and sacred that I didn't let you out of my arms for the first years of your life. I relished EVERY moment that I spent with you, marveling over who you were and every aspect of your development. It was the most golden kissed-by-God time imaginable. In your first years of life—in the backyard at Blanning—you would play your heart out; you were never done, always focused, always exploring, always "working" hard, and you only stopped to sleep! DA-NATTA!!!—as you would say when you were creating something great. And a few years later, "Mighty up the Fingers" was your cry when you were feeling the passion... for sword fighting or playing pirates.

One beautiful part of your story, Elijah, is that while it is unique, it's not a unique story. It's a piece of the larger story of all of us, in which we, as a people, are witness to many such moments of faith manifest.

Telling your twenty-year-old self over and over again that you were an answered prayer, a miracle even, may feel like a lot of pressure. (I mean, if you start as a miracle, where do you go from there?) It's why today I will remind you that while your story was miraculous, what's really important at this significant juncture in your life is to be a good steward of the faith that brought you here.

I have mothered you as best I know how, and of course I will continue to. But I know, as I watch you develop and stand before me as a man, that the blueprint is yours (and His), not mine. And while the story of your baby self can feel oh-so-beautiful and safe and very easily contained in a smaller world, I know your world today is vast and unknowable and will present, thankfully, with many challenges, which will also mean many opportunities for growth.

So yes, I've *temporarily* let go of the hand of older Elijah. I had to, as he has broken into a run. and I can't keep up, am not meant to keep up, with his long legs passing me long ago. In temporarily letting go, I released the illusion of you being mine, a baby belonging to a mother. For a time that may have been true, but you belong to something bigger now; you belong to yourself, you belong to the world, you belong to Him, and you are ready.

What I will not let go of is the faith that brought you here—and I know as I stand here, it will be this same faith that takes you through the journey of your adulthood, to the self that you were always destined to be.

When the man Elijah returns—as he has and as he will—to share funny stories, stories of victory and sadness, I'll be ready to grasp his larger hand in my two smaller ones. Yes, I'll be ready to marvel at the size of your hand in mine... at the calluses that have formed from your music, your dreams, your commitments, and from the many ways in which you have chosen to grow.

I don't know what life path you will ultimately choose, and the beautiful thing is, I don't have to. I know already *who you are and therefore who you will be.* I know you will continue to bring "better" to whatever is at hand. I know wherever you go, people will celebrate that you were there—and they will feel their lives were made far richer by knowing you.

Thinking of your future fills me with a sense of peace and optimism because I'm sure that you stand as ready and prepared for the world as you could ever be. Yet there is still an aspect of my love for you that will always be incredibly vulnerable, *because I love you so much.*

It's true that I have chosen not to show this to you many times, and I feel I should say I am sorry for hiding my tears when something mattered too much. Forgive me for not always being brave enough to show you the depths of my emotions. Oftentimes, I chose that because I did not want to burden you in the moment with my *big feelings.* However, this is who I am—an enormous feeler—and you know what? That's one way we are a lot alike!

I look at the young man you are today, and it tells me that we spent every minute as a family just as we should have. Remember as you go forth that the world needs and wants a Captain America, and that Christ is within you, so you need look no further. Look to your happy emotions to guide you to the path that God intends.

Be assured that I trust in who you are and the way that you, with a future as bright as the sun, will follow your heart to your rainbow's end, guitar in hand, friends abundant.

As you set forth, I hope only to tell you—in words that are worthy—what you have given to me by being the most beautiful son I could ever have imagined in my wildest dreams. I love every unique part of who you are: the beautiful, the brilliant, the soft, the hard, the vulnerable, the one who struggles at times as we all do. You do being human very well, and I'm so proud forever to be your mom.

Stay blue. Stay true. I wish you a million "DA-NATTA!" moments, Elijah.

And I'm not just mom-bragging when I tell you that your music is the only church I'll ever need and that it moves me to tears because it surpasses the beauty of truly all that I have known. Read that sentence again, please.

Maybe one day we'll get our zombie apocalypse, and you'll be the first one I'll seek.

I love you eternally,
Mom

2020 COVID-19 Snapshot: Making Art with Elijah for his art class with Mark Smith at Austin College—though decades apart, we shared the same college art instructor. Elijah's art is like his music... powerful, intense, effortless, brilliant in its simplicity of no wasted strokes. Elijah internalizes a lot, doesn't always speak out his processing. I've come to understand that he is the most intelligent person I know in all the ways that matter. I tell him that if there's a zombie apocalypse he is the first I will seek out. But let me tell you, he will survive it brilliantly!

Phoebe and Elijah

Elijah's graduation from Primary Montessori School

CHAPTER 24

Dear Sarah Katherine

Remembering, with love from Mom to Sarah Katherine on March 24, 2021.

Dear Sarah Katherine,

As I write this letter, I'm not in my usual place of peace and lightness, the place in my mind I would normally seek when wanting to bring forth the best reflections for such an important moment. But instead of resisting, I'm leaning into this moment, and the associated feelings, for the value that it offers to the task at hand.

And there is value, as I think about it, that I would be writing you from a place of more somber reflection. In truth, this is the place in which you will sit as you face certain situations in your future—those that will require decisions that are not easy, that will take the very best of your judgment-making skills. In your journeys ahead, the accomplishments you seek will, at times, require this.

Last night at dinner, Allison Schwartz and Amy Twomey asked about you. Again. I shared that you would be going to Hillsdale. Would Jake still be part of the equation? Yes, I answered. I told them that he planned to support you in whatever endeavors might be in your future, which will likely involve politics.

Allison offered feedback, spoken from the heart: she believed you will, in whatever position, *succeed in speaking up for and helping those that need it*, rather than just talking about it, as some would.

I thought that was a very true summation of your future, as it's also been a very accurate summation of your past. You've been a listener and a leader, always standing up for what is right and making things better, whether you were at White Rock Montessori or Bishop Lynch. Always making the work sacred by caring, stepping up, serving others, and doing the right thing.

Ms. Thacker from White Rock Montessori was right when she said during that lower elementary school parent-teacher conference so long ago that *in every situation, you and Elijah always knew the difference between right and wrong and acted accordingly.*

It's accurate that whatever action you're engaged in, you're always instinctively pointing yourself toward true north and doing it for the betterment of the group. Discerning what is just in every situation and then following it is your elemental nature. It's the switch that you can't turn off.

I love that it matters that much to you to do it right, always, and in everything. And while it's simple, I know that it's certainly not easy. I know your values will bring certain Abe Lincoln moments into your lifetime, in which you will be called to commit to a right way, even though it may be a less traveled path, even if sometimes it may feel downright solitary.

As I write this letter, of course, I don't have a crystal ball to know your future, but I *do* know that whatever you do, you'll do it in true Sarah Katherine fashion—far and above any expectations, while making the way better for others, with true north compass in hand.

I've told you that, since before you were born, I sensed your enormous strength, and I have witnessed others being drawn to you for that.

And they will continue to be drawn to you. Others will trust you and look to you to lead them, and you will undoubtedly have not only great influence but also great impact in whatever you undertake.

Undoubtedly, you'll change the world. In my heart I truly, truly know that you have a big place in history, a big place in our collective future. It's one of those things that all of us that know you feel . . . it's been a knowingness since you were little.

You're destined for great things. We've always known it. There is no one more capable, no one who was ever more ready for such a role. All the elements are there, Sarah Katherine.

And for this reason, you *will* have Abe Lincoln moments, during which you feel the weight of the country, the weight of the world, on your shoulders—and sometimes in those moments you may feel very, very alone. When those Abe Lincoln moments do come, Sarah Katherine, I pray that you may you know that the loneliness is there *so that you will turn to God.* And that through Him, you are strong enough for any challenge ahead. You are the best, most equipped of all of us.

In those moments, as you turn to Him and feel His presence, I pray you'll remember us, the family from which you have come—the good, the bad, the broken, and the beautiful, all of which have formed you into the very strong, remarkable person that you are today. I pray that you'll remember in those moments that there are no mistakes in God's kingdom—and all that you have been through, especially the challenges, has prepared you for the glorious future He intends for you.

And you know what else?

In those Abe Lincoln moments I pray mostly you'll remember the little girl who made you into the strong young woman you are today. Yes, please remember the sweet, sensitive, intelligent, funny, caring, creative, zany, fun-loving, very individualistic little girl who graced all of us with her presence . . . the one that made us want to hang onto every moment with her tiny, charming, larger-than-life, old-soul self.

After all, it was *her* courage that led you to the bar to squat your first plate, and it was *her* vulnerability that drove you to master the strength and confidence to transform from an intelligent, sensitive middle schooler into all that you would become: a high school cheerleader, a captain of the high school cheerleaders, a high school powerlifter, a captain of the high school powerlifters, a stellar high school student, and a captain of all of those stellar high school students.

Yes, Sarah Katherine, please remember to invite her sweet, frank, brave, true self when you are sitting in a somber Abe Lincoln moment, searching for a solution that may seem daunting, a solution so unreachable that it may seem not yet to exist. Remember her when the world seems upside down, when people are unyielding, because it will be her creativity and wisdom and sense of optimism that light your way through. Remember her in moments when it seems that hope has been lost, for I promise you she will show up faithfully, cheerfully, and capably. She will take your hand, and it will be her grace that leads you home.

Yes, remember her, give her a smile, show her your hand.

Remember who you are, remember her.

Always, always remember.

Because I will always remember. Always!

It's absolutely impossible for me to put into a letter, into a group of words, the vastness of my love for you. How could I begin to describe the happiness that you have brought me? How could I begin to tell you adequately that the sunny, golden days I have spent with you—raising you up, as your mother—have far surpassed the best of what I ever expected from joy?

How could I describe the perfection of experiencing mother-daughter companionship, the delight I felt in literally every moment in your company, because of your intelligent and loving observations? I cannot do justice to describing the pride I felt in watching all that you undertook, for it was always done with such aplomb and yielded such high results.

I won the mom lottery, that's for sure. Now I'm bragging, but I never understood why others were stressed out as young mothers. I am not exaggerating when I say it was the happiest, most enjoyable time of my life! It's what I was born to do: mother you and Elijah. You are both, without question, the great work of my lifetime (said humbly, all thanks to God!).

Being your mom has truly been the greatest happiness and blessing I've lived. Again, putting it into words is an impossibility. I would need music and some paints to show you even an inkling of what I really mean. Even so, I think it will only be possible for you to truly understand once you're a mother too!

Light up the world, Sarah Katherine. Your shine is too bright for most of us to look at directly. Shine anyway. Do it all. No one will be able to keep up but never, ever let it slow you down.

I love you forever, beyond the rainbow's end. You are all that my heart could have ever hoped for in a daughter.

Always,
Mom

Sarah Katherine, senior photo, Downtown Dallas

"I urge you to please notice when you are happy, and exclaim or murmur or think at some point, "If this isn't nice, I don't know what is."

"BUT WHAT I DO, I DO BECAUSE I LIKE TO DO."

These are Sarah Katherine's late-night creations during the COVID-19 pandemic.

Monday seemed to be a huge processing day for her. She was very emotional and didn't know why. I told her I thought she was mourning the plans she had made and invested in (for now and the immediate future). She managed herself well during quarantine, but it's true that we are all practicing the art of letting go of our old lives, in ways that we're not even aware of.

I'm glad to see her invest in her creative self; it's necessary always. After spending some time drawing late at night, she always emerges a brand-new person by morning.

Sarah Katherine's kindergarten years and first graduation

CHAPTER 25

Dear Teens and Parents

Teach Your Parents Well

Dear Teens,

It's been an honor and a privilege to work with you as a coach, mentor, and teacher. As you know, there's absolutely nothing easy about teenage years or high school—especially today. I've spent hours in prayer with and for many of you. I have witnessed your stresses and your tears and have heard the troubles of your hearts. I have seen firsthand the stresses that we adults have unwittingly created for your generation, how the dynamics of the world that we have influenced have brought you suffering in terms of mental health. I've also seen how adults—even those in positions of authority and teaching—downplay the impact of their collective actions, asking more from you than they themselves could ever produce or manage. Instead of showing mercy and understanding when you needed it, they faulted you for not doing enough. I know. I've sat in your circles. I've watched. I've seen it with my own eyes.

Maybe at one time in the world, around the 1950s, it was a more fulfilling and wholesome experience to be a teen, but today it is chaos. Every generation of parents is healing the ills of their own childhood (or choosing to ignore them), and in striving to do well for their kids, they over- or under-correct—unaware of the negative consequences of both. In this way, they recreate trauma and nudge you toward brands of parenting that will ensure you never want to repeat their mistakes.

I can't change the totality of the dynamics that have made you suffer in this moment; I would if I could, but I can't. So I primarily want to say I'm sorry for the state of things. It troubles me to sit with other educators and broach the subject of school shootings as they shrug their shoulders and say,

"Yeah, well, teens do crazy things."

Teens, I know none of you came into the world wanting to be stressed or wanting to be alienated from real-world situations in which you could truly be challenged to grow. I know that none of you wanted to turn to excess technology and medication to soothe yourselves when you couldn't forget or relax. And I know that none of you ever wanted to come into the world to harm another or to worry about being shot in the environment of your own school.

Parents, I will say to you—I know none of us wanted to create this kind of a world, but somehow, we did. It happened on our watch. What are we going to do to fix it?

Let's start with being aware of ourselves, our strengths, weaknesses, and tendencies as parents. Let's face it: those of us who were raised in the '70s, without enough parental input and oversight, became helicopter parents who wanted to make things perfect for our children, to eliminate the so-called dangers we were exposed to. This has resulted in our generation becoming parents who manipulate every last detail and give little freedom, forcing kids under a microscope, and imposing metrics on everything they do. It's not that we knew we were doing this, and unfortunately, we've realized too late that we have asked too much of our kids.

Unwittingly, we have given unlimited access and exposure to everything that technology brings instead of to the outdoors and the freedom they needed to accomplish things independently and gain confidence.

We have over-tested, over-manipulated, and overanalyzed every one of their actions to the point that they could not relax, then told them it was not enough. When they became overwhelmed with what we were asking, we acted as if it was their fault, rather than the fault of the environment, and we began to medicate them with drugs that had not been tested or proven to be beneficial. In fact, we gave them drugs that were not good for them—ones that could create suicidal ideations and aggressive tendencies. We did not monitor them once they started taking them. Then, when the well-intentioned drugs brought on negative side effects, we used this as evidence to prove they were flawed in the first place—reemphasizing the need for medication.

While all of the parental and societal input has been well-intentioned, it clearly has not always resulted in good circumstances for our children. And yet they all are highly emotionally intelligent as a population and will go on to do things better for their children, just as every generation does. As I write this, I know God's hand is behind the in-the-world influences that are bigger than all of us and that, later, in connecting the dots, we may have better insight into the purpose of the trials of each generation.

I want to remind our kids to trust their instincts and to choose accordingly. In turn, I share the following facts to encourage them, to help them understand that they have done their *very* best in *very* difficult circumstances. As they become adults and gain more control over their lives, I hope these stresses will fade and they will be able to create the reality of their own choosing.

In the United States, one of the greatest cultural priorities in preparing children for a promising future is selecting the best school available to them, so that they will, in turn, receive the best education. The collective dream of parents is to fulfill the blueprint of their child's human potential with learning that is meaningful, enriching, and rewarding. That's because, across the United States, our 77 million schoolchildren will spend an average of 16,380 hours in the classroom before graduating high school and beginning either college or a job.[10] That makes learning perhaps the single most important and time-consuming task that our nation's children will undertake in their young lives. Additionally, it is also the most stressful. In a recent survey by the APA, teen students aged thirteen to seventeen reported stress levels that were higher than adults... and far above what is considered healthy.[11]

Of teens polled, 36 percent reported feeling nervous or anxious; 31 percent reported feeling overwhelmed; and 30 percent reported feeling depressed or sad as a result of stress in the month prior to the survey.[12] Eighty-three percent of teens surveyed cited school as a source of stress, and sixty-nine percent cited "getting into a good college or deciding what to do after high school."

Stress levels in the classroom, by all indicators, begin at a young age. In fact, studies dating back to 1990 reveal the labeling of standardized testing for kindergartners as developmentally inappropriate practices and as potentially harmful.[13]

For over two decades, states have imposed standardized tests on schools as an external check on student progress under well-intentioned programs (No Child Left Behind) meant to help students' academic achievement.[14] And testing continues to be on the rise, especially in the last ten to fifteen years. A study from the Council of the Great City Schools found that students will take about 112 standardized tests from pre-K through twelfth grade.[15]

But ironically, the impact of this testing on learning has been largely negative due to test anxiety, poor morale, decreased comprehension, low confidence, and avoidance of school work.[16]

In fact, due to increased standardized testing, test anxiety has become the number one learning challenge of students today, affecting more than 10 million kids in North America.[17] More concerning, it has had troubling effects on the physical and emotional wellbeing of students.

In fact, as early as 2001, child psychiatrists, child development experts, and educators signed a statement advising against additional standardized testing, arguing that test-related stress is "literally making many children sick."[18]

This has revealed itself to be true in the evidences of test-related stress that manifest during periods of test administration, such as panic attacks, anxiety attacks, stomachaches, headaches, vomiting, sleep problems, depression, attendance problems, and acting out.[19]

Today, many sociologists and neuroscientists believe that regardless of ADHD's biological basis, the explosion in rates of diagnosis is caused by sociological factors, especially ones related to education and the changing expectations we have for kids.[20]

During the same thirty years when ADHD diagnoses increased, American childhood drastically changed. Kids now have more homework, less recess, and a lot less unstructured free time to relax and play. It's easy to now speculate how "ADHD" might have become a convenient societal catchall for what happens when kids are expected to be miniature adults.[21] For all of these reasons, it's important for school-aged children, including vulnerable teenagers, to understand the underlying causes of the stress they're experiencing.

As parents, our number one priority is for our children to be happy.

Children come into the world a perfect bundle of innocence, a perfect blueprint of humanity, a God-given package of pure potential for the future. But in a recent poll, 70 percent of our nation's adolescents claim that depression and anxiety are a major problem for them. In fact, according to HHA.gov, one in five adolescents has a diagnosable mental health disorder and at least one in three shows signs of depression.

Today, the youth suicide rate is the highest it's been since the government began collecting such statistics in 1960. Sadly, in the United States, suicide is the second leading cause of death among youths aged ten to nineteen years, with suicide rates increasing 33 percent between 1999 and 2014. For girls and young women, suicide rates have followed a steady upward trajectory with rates essentially doubling between 2000 and 2017. This means that the suicide rate for adolescent girls is now closer to the previously higher and problematic rate for boys.

As a parent today, I ask myself,

What went wrong?

How did this happen on our watch?

Who will fix this? If not us, who?

After doing some reading and research, I learned that psychotropic drug prescriptions for teenagers skyrocketed 250 percent between 1994 and 2001. Psychotropic drugs, incidentally, are drugs prescribed for mental health concerns such as depression and anxiety. I also learned that up to 60 percent of drug prescriptions in the US are "off-label," a sizable portion of which are written for children and adolescents.

Incidentally, *off-label* prescribing is both legal and common, and means that doctors have the option to prescribe medications to teens in a manner not specified in the FDA's approved packaging label.

The WebMD website describes what many people may be surprised to know: the FDA regulates drug approval, not drug prescribing, and therefore, doctors are free to prescribe a drug for any reason they think is medically appropriate.

So that is how, in many cases, drugs prescribed to teens have not been FDA approved for use by adolescents. And why are they not approved? Because of a lack of research. On their website, a spokesman from the US Food and Drug Administration claims that "we need more pediatric studies because many antidepressants approved for adults have not been proven to work in kids."[22]

Myth: Children are little adults.

Truth: An adolescent's developing brain is vulnerable and different from an adult's.

We DO know that many psychotropic drugs prescribed to teens are disturbing the normal process of the adolescent brain. In fact, in 2003, the FDA issued public warnings that taking antidepressants increases the risk of suicidality (defined as serious thoughts about taking one's own life or planning or attempting suicide) among children, adolescents, and young adults.[23]

Why is this information not common knowledge today? Perhaps because these highly publicized warnings, which continued through 2008, resulted in a 50 percent decline in the use of antidepressants among teens. Coincidentally, during this same time period there was also a decline in teen suicide.

For whatever reason, the highly publicized warnings from the FDA stopped in 2008.

Still, we see cautions, such as the one on the Mayo Clinic website that advertises to watch for suicide attempts in our adolescents in the first few months of antidepressant treatment.[24]

Parents, I say to you that in the United States the history of mental health for our teens is complex, and answers are not easy. But is this something we can afford not to investigate? If we know as a society that our children are suffering to this degree, what will it take for us adults to finally address the issue? And what if the damage we are doing extends beyond the school years?

What if we are actually doing the opposite of preparing them for a successful future?

What then?

Additionally, there are medications for *everything*...from depression and anxiety to ADHD and insomnia. Drugs are being prescribed in alarming numbers across the country, but the "cure" is often worse than the original problem. *Medication Madness* by Dr. Peter R. Breggin is a fascinating, frightening, and dramatic look at the role that psychiatric medications have played in fifty cases of suicide, murder, and other violent, criminal, and bizarre behaviors.

As a psychiatrist who believes in holding people responsible for their conduct, Dr. Breggin was eventually convinced by the weight of scientific evidence and years of clinical experience that psychiatric drugs frequently cause individuals to lose their judgment and their ability to control their emotions and actions. *Medication Madness* raises and examines the issues surrounding personal responsibility when behavior seems driven by drug-induced adverse reactions and intoxication.

Dr. Breggin personally evaluated the cases in the book in his role as a treating psychiatrist, consultant, or medical expert. He interviewed survivors and witnesses and reviewed extensive medical, occupational, educational, and police records. The great majority of individuals examined lived exemplary lives and committed no criminal or bizarre actions prior to taking the psychiatric medications.

Medication Madness reads like a medical thriller, true crime story, and courtroom drama, but it is firmly based in the latest scientific research and dozens of case studies. The lives of the children and adults in these stories, as well as the lives of their families and their victims, were thrown into turmoil and sometimes destroyed by the unanticipated effects of psychiatric drugs. In some cases, our entire society was transformed by the tragic outcomes. Many categories of psychiatric drugs can cause potentially horrendous reactions.[25]

Prozac, Paxil, Zoloft, Adderall, Ritalin, Concerta, Xanax, lithium, Zyprexa, and other psychiatric medications may spellbind patients into believing they are improved when too often they are becoming worse. Psychiatric drugs drive some people into psychosis, mania, depression, suicide, agitation, compulsive violence, and loss of self-control without the individuals realizing that their medications have deformed their way of thinking and feeling.

This book documents how the FDA, the medical establishment, and the pharmaceutical industry have oversold the value of psychiatric drugs. It serves as a cautionary tale about our reliance on potentially dangerous psychoactive chemicals to relieve our emotional problems and provides a positive approach to taking personal charge of our lives.

Apology to the Teens

Sorry.
It happened on our watch.
Dismayed. Afraid. You paid. We stayed.
In denial. Not ours. Then whose?

*This shadow gift (*Don't you want it?*) that we bequeathed.*
That was our legacy. Your legacy.
No wonder trust was lost.

(In truth), we lost that first, not last.
No wonder you stopped viewing us as adults
In charge.

The past. It has. To mean something.

Because we were not grown-ups,
You did not get to be kids.
Santa's coming.
With a bottle of fix.
End the tricks.

Thank God.
We didn't create kids who were born to do this.
Thank God.
Our sin was alienation. Forsaking self.

Not knowing the fix was within.
Doing the easy. Washing our hands.
Playing with fire.
Creating an easy way out.

One for you. One for me. Pills, see?
Change our reality.
Looking away when the guns went off,
Pointing fingers when it was our fingers
On the trigger.

The good news is too many pills is fixable.
Hearts can be mended.
We can learn to be there.
Show our hurt. Speak our truth. Love.
Can you fix broken people?
God can.
We must.
In Him we trust.

Time to show our ass.
Be real. Own up. Pay now.
Let the children be.
Restore innocence—like past tense.
Raise rents.
Break open the spiritual toolbox.
Hammer out loud. Forgive.

Sorry?
Only God can know how much.
His touch. A balm. No bombs.
Right wrongs.

Child, how you doin' in this modern world?

20/20. No more choosing not to see.

Looking back to see ahead.
Let's wed. No more dead.

You on board?

Spread the word. Cuz I've heard.
Broken is okay. Cuz we all are.
Just need to join hands. Make plans.
Be friends.

Make a love chain. No weak links.
Weaklings.
Wounded healers. Heal each other through our wounds.
What if I promised to be there
Next time you did not want to choose the future?
Next time what if we did not choose avoidance? Convenience?
Pretending?

What if we chose to walk through our hurt with no shirt?
In the dirt.
Back to who we are.

Tell myself I'm coming.

No sorry big enough.
No tough, enough.
Right stuff.

Can't bring them back.
But what can we do in their name?

I'm not asking you to do anything more than spend
five minutes
Investing in a new truth.

I lost a mom who was too sad.
So sad, too bad.
Came off her lithium fast, no repast.
Delusions set in, the end.

Lost a brother.
24-hour hallucinations.
But still he had a voice of reason.
He tried, but died.
The pills, they helped him.

Jesus.
Sees us.
Would it please us
For him to be the one that
Frees us?

If you got a better idea,
Let's hear it.
Get near it.

Pills are not divine.
They screw the mind.
Don't mind?
I mind.

Don't take the shortcut.
Quit the pills. Face your ills.
Pay the bills.
No frills.

Choose. To love your shoes.
Leave the blues.
Body as a temple.

I will love you broken.
Not just a token.
No truer words spoken.

Just need the music.
So you can sing my song
Leave the wrong
Keep us strong

Randy Weaver
Had no fever
Got a wife
And couldn't keep her.

CHAPTER 26

Dear Veterans

Dear Veterans,

Kevin and I both served on active duty as Marines from 1988 through 1992, during the first Persian Gulf crisis, and our service afterward consisted of several years of reserve duty. In some ways, being young lieutenants serving during the same era of history meant that we had common experiences. But because we are opposite genders, were placed within units of differing missions, and have unique personality traits that individually define us, we had experiences that were also very different from one another. Nevertheless, as we see it, during our service we were unified in marriage and unified by the United States Marine Corps, which has been promoting peace and stability across the globe since its inception.

On more than one occasion, Kevin and I have discussed the *ordinariness* of our time in the service. It sometimes feels strange to relay our experiences to a civilian who hopes for a story of heroism. Instead, we feel that our story is one of two officers whose service, albeit during a time of war, did not denote the remarkable.

Yet in truth, if you were to ask those who have served, especially those who have been named as heroes, you would likely find that they view their service in the same light as we view ours—*we were just doing our jobs*. As American Admiral Halsey, who served in the United States Navy during WWII, stated, "There are no great men. There are only great challenges, which ordinary men like you and me are forced by circumstances to meet."

Halsey's quote may seem to fly in the face of the reverence and respect that we crave to bestow on those who have shown themselves to be heroes during times of war, but upon closer inspection it's evident that Halsey's statement is an accurate representation of what they believe about their own service. While at first glance it may seem to detract from the accolades we would like to extend to them, it is actually a statement of enormous respect to our heroes in that it recognizes their own manner of thinking.

Just as important, it is also a statement that unconditionally extends to all who serve and recognizes that they, given the same circumstances, would rise to the same extraordinary outcome. This is perhaps the reason why Kevin and I choose to share our experiences. Because in the telling of our *less than remarkable story*, which includes the stories of others who have served, we are observing the fascinating bridge where *the ordinary* meets miracles—the inexplicable link that has yielded extraordinary acts of heroism and emphasizes the supreme sacrifices many have made.

We must consider first that since the birth of our United States on July 4, 1776, no single generation of Americans has been spared the responsibility of defending liberty by force of arms; more than 42 million American men and women have served in a time of war;

and more than one million have given the ultimate sacrifice—their lives—in defense of such liberty.

As a nation that has known relative peace, it is important to recognize the millions who have served during times of both recognized and unrecognized conflict to preserve that peace. Incidents like the Beirut bombing or the tragedy that befell the *USS Cole* remind us that all who serve, even in times of peace, do so at the risk of life.

It is important to note, then, that what makes a veteran is not a National Defense Medal earned during wartime, nor is it the uniform itself. It is the willingness and readiness that marks us, the idea that we are trained and prepared, that we stand ready, as ordinary citizens, in the event that duty calls. Duty *did call*—to Kevin and me—and so we served, yielding circumstances that we overcame, though they caused some of the most painful memories of our marriage.

On January 14, 1991, while pregnant and on active duty, after weeks of prolonged bleeding and pain, I drove myself to the Camp Lejeune Naval Hospital emergency room to be seen. I had been denied access to a doctor—despite my tears and urgings throughout the previous day—and had called all civilian medical facilities in the area, only to be told that they would not be able to see me because I was under the jurisdiction of the military. Finally, at midnight, I concluded that the only way I would be able to see a doctor was to report to the emergency room, so I did.

Kevin was deployed at the time and because there was no real means of communication besides Red Cross messages, he wasn't even aware that I was pregnant yet.

Upon arrival, after describing my symptoms and history, the attending physician in the emergency room was horrified to hear I had been denied the ability to see a doctor. I had been bleeding for several weeks, been experiencing pain, and had abnormal BHCG counts. Despite my previous three visits to an on-site clinic, there were no medical steps taken to further examine me other than my exam by a PA. I was told this was due to *protocol*, because the baby wasn't far enough along for a visit with an MD.

After reporting to the emergency room, I was prepped immediately for surgery for a ruptured tubal pregnancy, and when they asked who they could notify, I told them they could call my sister Mary, who had moved to Camp Lejeune, North Carolina, to be near me. The surgery revealed that my tube had indeed ruptured and that, over previous days, I had already lost ten percent of my blood, which had pooled in my peritoneal cavity. During the operation, bleeding was persistent and hard to control, and consequently they had to remove half of my left fallopian tube.

After surgery, one of the medical staff told me that had I not driven myself to the emergency room that night, I likely would have gone into shock in my sleep and died. They also told me that my two post-op EKGs showed a first-degree AV block. Over the next several days, the reports inexplicably "disappeared." My guess is that no one in the medical chain of command wanted to explain my newly non-deployable status to the powers that be. I had neither the energy, courage, nor trust to pursue the matter further and was discharged from the hospital with a mandatory forty-two days of convalescent leave. With Kevin deployed to the Persian Gulf, it would be some time before he found out about my surgery and the lost pregnancy.

Without really intending to do so, I put my grief on hold. There was a war going on and Kevin was in the middle of it. Additionally, without being able to talk to him about what privately belonged to the two of us, I found it most natural to not speak about it much at all. I'd found out I was pregnant shortly after Kevin had been deployed. I was overjoyed because, although we wanted a baby, so far in our marriage I had not become pregnant. My joy was punctuated by a fearful thought that hovered as well: perhaps God was giving me a baby because Kevin wasn't coming home.

Kevin did return home, but not until almost half a year later. Couples who have experienced deployment, especially during a time of very limited communication options, will acknowledge that important matters get put on the back burner. Even when the loved one arrives back home, there are significant adjustments that must be addressed—such as learning to live together again. Often there are too many critical topics to address all at once, with no real way of prioritizing. For some couples, the lid blows off, resulting in divorce. In our case, we simply walked around a subject that was too big for both of us, especially as new daily priorities were presented. It wasn't necessarily a healthier option, it's just what we chose by default as a means of coping.

The pain didn't go away, though. Nor did the enormous feelings of anxiety that built up as a result of the incident. They both just got buried—and for me would not completely surface for another thirty years, although aspects of my experience would manifest themselves in certain decisions, such as avoiding doctors at all costs for years and years. When I did become pregnant, I birthed at a birth center with midwives and no doctors present, except for the one on call for emergencies.

Kevin's pain was hidden and invisible to me—and likely to himself as well—and I can't speak to the ways in which it manifested for him. This is true except for the repeated dreams that continue to visit, even today, and that require me to wake him quickly and firmly, then move away from his sleeping, thrashing, fighting, yelling form for my own safety.

Inside of me, the pain that I wasn't willing to face waited. In limited ways over the years, I grieved intermittently for my unborn child; for the deferred hope of motherhood; for all the loss I'd suffered as the daughter of a mother who had passed, and now the mother of a child whom I would never hold. But in true military fashion, I put the pain into a compartment and pushed forward, never looking back as I completed my service. It took years to fully grasp the scope of how traumatic the experience was; even now it surfaces. In many ways it feels like someone else's memory or dream, like it didn't belong to me but plagues my psyche in ways I do and do not know.

After I turned fifty-three, a sergeant major inspired me to call the VA to discuss my emergency ectopic pregnancy. I was shocked at the divine synchronicity that presented. The representative I spoke with was also a female veteran who had likewise experienced a life-threatening ectopic pregnancy as a civilian. Similar to my situation, her doctor had neglected to properly diagnose her. Come to find out, her mother had undergone a hysterectomy at age thirty-nine and subsequently became mentally ill—just like my mother.

The representative concluded,

"It wasn't my mother's fault—they took her ovaries; of course, she became crazy."

It made me realize that my mother was not to blame for her erratic behavior—here was an uncanny example of a woman who had suffered identically from the same scenario. In fact, the representative went on to share that her upbringing was a Beaver Cleaver story... the perfect childhood... that is, until her mother's hysterectomy.

Her story concluded in her describing her adult life as not what she envisioned, not what she imagined or hoped for as a single mom of three children. Furthermore, she believed that her time in the Army was detrimental and, in part, caused the unhappy outcome.

The juxtaposition and irony of our stories was not lost on me. We had suffered identical mother wounds, in the context of different family-of-origin scenarios, and with very different parenting outcomes for each of us. The Army was a shortfall in her story, while the Marine Corps was a building block in mine.

Our conversation made me realize that we bear our pain as mothers and daughters universally, and that sometimes, when we surrender our lives to the military, we are not aware of the price of being too strong. As I think of the service men and women in our country, I believe it is essential to recognize faith as the key ingredient to our remarkable military. If our goal as a country is spiritual unity and oneness, we must pledge to forevermore see the training of our service people as a spiritual task, where they are broken down as individuals and rebuilt as a unit in which they identify with a higher purpose.

God calls us by saying, "Come to Me broken in spirit." Bootcamp serves to break our egos until we submit, until we are formed again full of spiritual wisdom for the goal of eternal service and the greater good of mankind. Through many seasons of loss, my fellow service members demonstrate an eternal cycle of loyalty, respect, caretaking, and sacrifice for all of us. They are selflessly devoted to a higher cause—one that exists to defend their faith, their families, and their freedom. They will continue to be unconcerned with personal cost—that is, until the day they are forced to face it. In those moments, I pray for them all, pray that they may reach out and take hold of God's peace as they patiently navigate the healing, and subsequent growth, that He intends for each of them. In time, God willing, all will be made whole again.

I give thanks and respect from the deepest part of my heart to each and every person who has been called to wear the uniform for the United States, recognizing that our inherent worthiness has been larger defined by the ordinariness that we pledge to commit in sometimes extraordinary ways—to the beautiful body and spirit of our military as a people, as a whole. Semper Fi.

Young lieutenants, photo taken at Camp Lejeune following the original Persian Gulf conflict

Getting married in 1989 at the Stafford County courthouse by a justice of the peace was a really good decision with money being limited… and us about to receive orders that could've landed us on opposite coasts.

Being witnessed by Kevin's roommate and his wife, it was as sacred as any ceremony could have been (I'm forever grateful to her for bringing a camera!), just as a chocolate shake at Denny's afterward was a great, low-stress way to celebrate.

No, nothing was missing on the day we wed, Kevin, because you were there and I was there, and we both carried God in our hearts, as well as the blueprint that He had for us, which has led to this perfect day that He has made. I do… and always will. Love you forever. Forever and ever, Amen!

Some of the female officer candidates of Charlie 4. Only 40 percent of us made it through training. The beautiful bright spark to the far right was my bunkie, Jodi Moore, who took her life once she got to the Fleet Marine Force. None of us knew she was struggling. We need to watch for our "strong" brothers and sisters especially.

Quantico Sentry

July 24, 1987

TAGS hosts Corps-wide conference

This is from Officer Candidate School 1987, taken at the top of the twenty-foot rope climb on the well-known USMC obstacle course (we had to yell out "Marine Corps" before descending).

Feels so differently to look at this today than it did then.

Now I find I am looking at myself through the lens of a tribal elder, rather than a self-critic, and I feel pride on behalf of the young gal who came from a family of artists and made her way through an environment that was initially very foreign to her.

Even though I was not possessed of a very tactical mind, I grew to love the people above all and had a flourishing short career. I still have very vivid dreams about the Marine Corps, and I wonder today what it would've been like had I stayed the full twenty... part of me really wishes I had.

This was me on January 16, 1991, during the original Persian Gulf conflict. The person pictured with me is another (then) USMC lieutenant— a fellow supply officer who was my sister's boyfriend at the time. My sister took this picture. Just two days before this photo was taken, I was at work in my office for Initial Issue Provisioning, 2nd Supply Battalion, 2nd FSSG, Camp Lejeune, North Carolina. We had just finished a big effort to ship all rolling stock from the East Coast to SWA. At the time of this photo, Kevin was deployed to the Persian Gulf and our communication was limited to Red Cross messages; thus he had yet to find out about my pregnancy and emergency surgery.

Me, getting sworn in to the Texas State Guard.

I had no idea what to expect!

Me, pictured with other TXSG personnel in a meeting with the Navarro County Office of Emergency Management.

Lieutenant Before Marriage Portrait

Texas State Guard Portrait, age fifty-four

Most definitely a thrilling moment to go to TXSG Annual Training and meet my Allred cousin for the first time ever! I saw Jimmy Allred's name in a Texas State Guard email and knew we must be related. We were! As I was entering the TXSG, he was retiring. I pledged to carry on in his good name... the name of our Allred Family!

I had the privilege of teaching a class on spiritual mentoring to the leadership of the Texas State Guard. Due to all that's happening in the world today, and the dynamics of the class, there was an opportunity to speak deeply on matters of the heart. The experience was a standout for me, and I was amazed to observe the safety and trust created in the room based upon the willingness of strong leaders to share. What I learned at this conference, above all, is that when the strong among us are willing to demonstrate being vulnerable, then the rest of us know it's okay to be vulnerable too. Maybe the healing comes when we are willing to cry in front of each other. Maybe that's what has been missing all of this time.

(Photos above and below taken by/used with permission of TXSG Public Affairs Officer WO1 Kevin Farley)

CHAPTER 27

Dear Phoebe, the Day Is Good

Dear Elijah,

You have often said, sometimes tearfully, that you wished to meet my mother, your Grandmommy Pope as we called her when you were little.

I submit to you that you have already, for she exists within you—and you have taken the best of all her creativity to bring us music more beautiful than I could ever have conceived. Your imagination is an inspiration, and I will always remember your cry when sword-fighting as a little one—to "Mighty up the Fingers!"

In fact, we adopted your phrase as the name of the summer camp we hosted at our house for your friends at White Rock Montessori. We wrote a play about Olaf the Giant, dressed up as characters, and invited the parents—my friends—to the final performance.

Dear Sarah Katherine,

When you dreamed repeatedly of my mother in your younger years, when she came to you and you realized that she was not "passed on" at all as we thought, I submit that your dream represented the spiritual truth that she lives on in both you and Elijah... and in all of us. Just as our ancestors do.

And she's been here, all this time, with us all along, just as God has been here within us, as close as our own breath.

May we all choose, as we move forward in time, as we move toward the ever after, as we move toward eternal love, may we choose all our days to be good.

In His name. Forever and ever, Amen.

For Elijah and Sarah Katherine

By Phoebe Sisk

Remember as you look upon yourself,
The day is good.
Happiness belongs to us here, now.
Peace is what we choose.

Remember as you look upon yourself,
Do so with love.
Gaze deeply into your own eyes and see your
Best self reflected there.

Love as much as you know how, for it is circular, hold nothing back.
Forgive as many times as people you know. Then forgive again.

Remember as you look upon yourself, the answer lies waiting
Before the question arises.

Love as much as you know how.

The day is good.

The Day Is Good

"The Day Is Good," he said to me,
Three-year-old eyes steady to mine;
The purest blue.

"The Day Is Good," and I know that, for him,
Our morning of playing on the stairs landing
Has measured up;

That in the morning of pretending,
Just me, him, and his little sister
A new mark has been made—
A wholeness achieved.

Just on the landing together—
In tying his cape, forming my body as a bridge;

Being willing to play the bad guy—

I understand that we have, together, for just a moment
Made grace for mankind.

Elijah and Sarah Katherine at the Dallas World Aquarium

I think of "Gone From My Sight" by Henry Van Dyke when I see this photo of the three of us . . . I imagine that we are standing on the seashore, watching as the ship, an object of beauty and strength, spreads her white sails and then becomes a speck where sky meets sea . . . Just as we, on this shore, acknowledge that she is gone, gone from our sight, other eyes and voices on another horizon are watching, ready to shout "Here she comes!"

Three generations of women

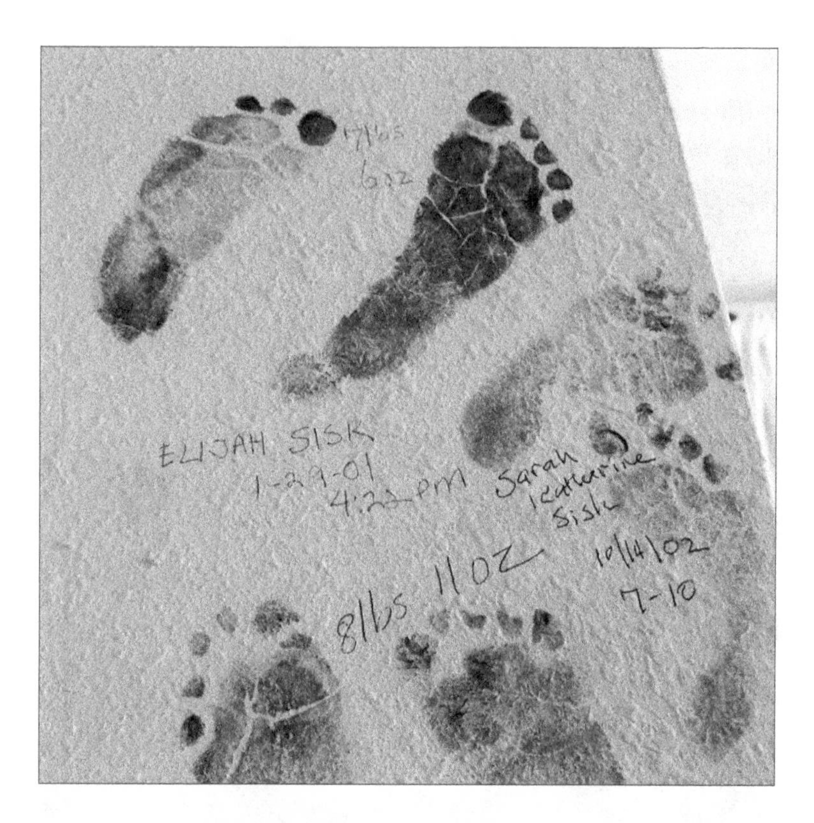

Elijah's and Sarah Katherine's footprints at the Dallas Women's and Birthing Center

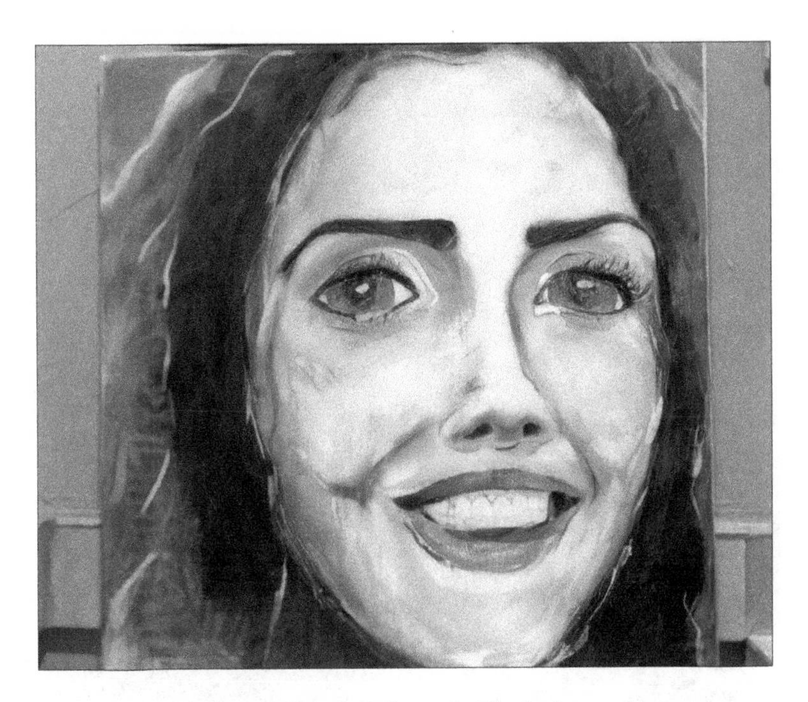

A painting of Sarah Katherine by Phoebe during the 2020 COVID-19 pandemic

A painting of Elijah by Phoebe during the 2020 COVID-19 pandemic

AFTERWORD

For Phoebe: Kevin's Story

Well, I picked up eighteen years into her story. September 1985 to be exact.

Phoebe was a new transfer student at Austin College, and I was beginning my second year there. She was eighteen, and I was nineteen.

Besides being shockingly beautiful and amazingly easy to talk to, she was wicked smart, funny, thoughtful, sincere, and humble. I use these attributes now—thirty-six years later—to describe what my nineteen-year-old conscious brain could not comprehend, but my subconscious most certainly did.

I was overwhelmed that this stunningly beautiful, funny, smart young lady was communicating with me! At first, I'm thinking she's being nice, you know, going easy on the *border-town kid*... until Superman comes along, making it so obvious that even the *border-town* kid would recognize his defeat and surrender without challenge.

But I stayed in pursuit, and she kept communicating... and eventually, she started to reveal the circles. Very, very slowly, but reveal she did. It wasn't days or weeks or even months, but years.

Little did I know what life Phoebe had already lived the moment we first met. How could I? How could anyone? She wasn't even clear (then) about how her journey and experiences were foundational in her character. She was living and pursuing excellence to create what she never had—normalcy.

The path through which she found full assimilation into that elusive *regular* world was academic excellence. Phoebe was unrelenting on this front.

A different journey, or a more traditional one, might have kept our paths from crossing at all. She was somebody that could and did have the attention of any young man she wanted. She had lots of girlfriends too. Everybody wanted to be around Phoebe—and that's still true to this day. I was the opposite of that. But I'm certain her journey gave her the insight and ability to connect with all kinds of people in a genuine and authentic way—a way that makes you feel special and heard. Phoebe is a great listener and always asks great questions.

Oddly, I'm convinced this is a skill Phoebe developed early on. It is what gave a kid like me any chance at all to win her for life. But I assure you, it was only a chance. I had to earn my way into her story. Guarded isn't the right description. We guard brownies and ice cream. Phoebe's story was nonexistent—almost like she was born at eighteen and all the rest didn't exist.

My saving virtue was an unwillingness to quit on her. There were times when she pushed me away—hard... and with forever in my mind. But I wouldn't let go. I'm no sage, nor did I profess to have had any great understanding back then—I didn't. I only had my instincts that told me her running away from me was not really her goal. They were just episodes of delaying my getting close to her.

Still, each one of those episodes (and there were many) brought me in closer and closer. Not by deliberate intention—but simply because each layer peeled and revealed my being safe to Phoebe. Episodes of her trying to get rid of me led to my unwillingness to quit her . . . and this made us each more certain about the other.

We were (and still are) wildly in love. We've spent every second together possible. Those episodes, although real and numerous, were a necessary part of forging the relationship. She had to know she could trust me . . . and the only way I could prove it was to always be there.

For a young girl growing up, someone showing up unconditionally and without guilt was nonexistent to her. Phoebe had to know my love was unconditional . . . so I set out to prove it.

I still like to introduce her as my girlfriend of thirty-six years—because we keep it the way it's always been. But I couldn't be prouder that she's my wife, partner, and best friend of more than three decades—and the mother of our two beautiful, thoughtful, and caring children—Elijah and Sarah Katherine.

The mother she is to them is the mother Phoebe never knew. The mythical shadow that Phoebe lived under for decades has been eclipsed by the mother she has truly become.

Let the story reign!

Unswervingly Yours,
Kevin

A Letter from Sarah Katherine to Her Mother, Phoebe

Mom,

It is both a challenge and an honor to try to articulate all that you are to me, to Dad, to Elijah, and to the world—as a woman in your own right.

Throughout the nineteen years that I have been alive, I have learned so much from you. Most of it has not been from explicit lessons but rather through watching you. You never needed to reprimand or lecture, because you have always respected me and Elijah. Even when we were young kids, you were intentional, always believing that we could rise to the occasion. And so, we naturally hold the deepest respect for you.

It is not within your person to do something half-heartedly. From the Marine Corps, to working, to volunteering at our schools, to raising us, you threw every ounce of your being into whatever needed to be done—without regard to personal gain or recognition. You have been the most excellent example of unconditional love and service, as Jesus did for us. You represent true servant leadership.

I am so happy that you are writing this book and finally getting to do something for yourself. You, of all people, deserve it.

I could list your many great accomplishments, but I think that would take a while, and detract from my point. The most important thing you have taught me is what a good mother looks like. In a world that is increasingly losing appreciation for the grit that motherhood (and fatherhood) requires, you have made me realize that the most important thing in my life is family.

You filled our house with so many magical experiences—fostering our creativity and curiosity. You let us have bad days (for me, more often than I will admit) and validated our feelings. You never missed a show, game, recital, or any other ceremony. You even flew to Michigan for my first game cheering in college.

Like you, I have always had big aspirations. You have managed them, all while being a full-time mom and wife. However, because of the model you have set for me, my biggest aspiration is to be a mom, just like you. All the other stuff can come as God sees fit.

From the time I was old enough to comprehend just how little you were when you lost your mama, I always wondered how you did it. Growing up without *yours*, how is it that you knew exactly how to be *my* mom? It is truly a beautiful thing.

I cry for the little girl who lost her mom because I cannot understand the heartbreak.

I know you had loving siblings and a great dad who all cared deeply, but I know it could not have been the same.

You had every right to be mad. At the world, at God, but that is not the kind of person my mother is.

So thank you, Mom, for giving me something I know you did not get.

Thank you for giving me a safe place to call home, for giving me everything I could ever need or want, and for loving me always.

I'll love you forever,
Sarah Katherine

A Note from Elijah to Mom, Phoebe

Mom, fifty-five! What a year to be alive. Mother, Hero, Life Giver! I hope that this day is more than a celebration of age and is also a celebration of all that you have dreamed, manifested, and brought to life during your time on this Earth. You have an eternity of things to be proud of. If I can ever be half the person you are, then perhaps I will be able to rest easy someday. You are my role model and my real-life superwoman. I am always here, always on your side, and always your son.

I love you forever. Happy birthday, Mom. Here is a synopsis of the ALL MOZART concert we will be attending on 3/5/2022. Pick out your best dress and let's head to the dance. CAN'T WAIT!

ENDNOTES

[1] Mark Wolynn, *It Didn't Start with You: How Inherited Family Trauma Shapes Who We Are and How to End the Cycle* (New York: Viking, 2016).

[2] *Desperate Crossing: The Untold Story of the Mayflower*, directed by Lisa Quijano Wolfinger, produced by Lone Wolf Documentary Group, 2006, https://watch.historyvault.com/specials/desperate-crossing-the-untold-story-of-the-mayflower.

[3] Wikipedia, s.v., "Rollo," last modified June 7, 2022, 00:22, https://en.wikipedia.org/wiki/Rollo.

[4] Yu-Chih Shen, et al., "Association of Hysterectomy with Bipolar Disorder Risk: A Population-Based Cohort Study," *Depression and Anxiety* 36, no. 6 (June 2019): 543–51. https://pubmed.ncbi.nlm.nih.gov/31025812/.

[5] "Hysterectomy Associated with Increased Risk of Bipolar Disorder, Study Suggests," *Psychiatric News*, May 6, 2019, https://alert.psychnews.org/2019/05/hysterectomy-associated-with-increased.html.

[6] Diane Ridaeus, "Lithium Withdrawal Symptoms, Side Effects, Treatment Help," *Alternative to Meds Center* (blog), last modified February 15, 2022, https://www.alternativetomeds.com/blog/lithium/; "Lithium Withdrawal Symptoms: List of Possibilities," *Mental Health Daily* (blog), accessed November 29, 2021, https://mentalhealthdaily.com/2014/04/24/lithium-withdrawal-symptoms-list-of-possibilities/.

[7] Sam McCulloch, "Twilight Sleep—The Brutal Way Some Women Gave Birth in the 1900s," *BellyBelly*, last modified May 31, 2022, https://www.bellybelly.com.au/birth/twilight-sleep/.

[8] J. Sinclair Armstrong, et al., "21st Annual Report of the Securities and Exchange Commission: Fiscal Year Ended June 30, 1955," Securities and Exchange Commission, March 30, 1956, http://3197d6d14b5f19f2f440-5e13d29c4c016cf96cbbfd197c579b45.r81.cf1.rackcdn.com/collection/papers/1950/1955_0630_SECAR.pdf; "Oran Henderson Allred," *Prabook*, accessed November 29, 2021, https://prabook.com/web/oran_henderson.allred/1458360.

[9] Allen Johnson, "Tetanus—Are You at Risk?," North Dakota Department of Health, last modified April 10, 1997, accessed November 29, 2021, https://www.ndhealth.gov/Publications/prevent/tetanus/tetanus.htm.

[10] "Census Bureau Reports Nearly 77 Million Students Enrolled in US Schools," United States Census Bureau, December 3, 2019, https://www.census.gov/newsroom/press-releases/2019/school-enrollment.html.

[11] Christina Simpson, "Effect of Standardized Testing on Students' Well-Being," Harvard Graduate School of Education, May 2016, https://projects.iq.harvard.edu/files/eap/files/c._simpson_effects_of_testing_on_well_being_5_16.pdf.

[12] Simpson, "Effect of Standardized Testing."

[13] Pamela Owen Fleege, "Stress Begins in Kindergarten: A Look at Behavior During Standardized Testing," Louisiana State University and Agricultural & Mechanical College, 1990, https://digitalcommons.lsu.edu/cgi/viewcontent.cgi?article=5911&context=gradschool_disstheses.

[14] Andrew M.I. Lee, "What is No Child Left Behind (NCLB)?" Understood, accessed July 8, 2022, https://www.understood.org/en/articles/no-child-left-behind-nclb-what-you-need-to-know.

[15] Stacy Tornio, "More Kids Than Ever Are Dealing with Test Anxiety, and We Need to Help," *WeAreTeachers* (blog), March 14, 2019, https://www.weareteachers.com/test-anxiety/.

[16] Tornio, "More Kids Than Ever Are Dealing with Test Anxiety."

[17] Tornio, "More Kids Than Ever Are Dealing with Test Anxiety."

[18] Simpson, "Effect of Standardized Testing."

[19] Simpson, "Effect of Standardized Testing."

[20] Maggie Koerth-Baker, "The Not-So-Hidden Cause Behind the ADHD Epidemic," *New York Times*, October 15, 2013, https://www.nytimes.com/2013/10/20/magazine/the-not-so-hidden-cause-behind-the-adhd-epidemic.html.

[21] Koerth-Baker, "The Not-So-Hidden Cause."

[22] Kelli Miller, "Off-Label Drug Use: What You Need to Know," *WebMD*, accessed June 7, 2022, https://www.webmd.com/a-to-z-guides/features/off-label-drug-use-what-you-need-to-know.

[23] "Suicidality in Children and Adolescents Being Treated With Antidepressant Medications," US Food and Drug Administration, February 5, 2018, https://www.fda.gov/drugs/postmarket-drug-safety-information-patients-and-providers/suicidality-children-and-adolescents-being-treated-antidepressant-medications.

[24] "Antidepressants for Children and Teens," Mayo Clinic, March 19, 2022, https://www.mayoclinic.org/diseases-conditions/teen-depression/in-depth/antidepressants/art-20047502.

[25] Peter Breggin, *Medication Madness: The Role of Psychiatric Drugs in Cases of Violence, Suicide, and Crime* (New York: St. Martin's Griffin, 2009).

CPSIA information can be obtained
at www.ICGtesting.com
Printed in the USA
BVHW070758110922
646359BV00002B/11